MORE SCRAMBLES

IN THE

LAKE DISTRICT

One of the many slabby craglets on Red Pike, Wasdale (Route 65)

MORE SCRAMBLES

IN THE

LAKE DISTRICT

R.Brian Evans

Illustrations by the author
except where stated

CICERONE PRESS
MILNTHORPE, CUMBRIA

> # WARNING!
> ## SCRAMBLING CAN BE DANGEROUS.

ACKNOWLEDGEMENTS

My thanks are due to all those people who told me about their favourite scrambles, not listed in the original guidebook. Special thanks go to the Lake District artist, Jim Riley, whose fell wanderings are rarely straightforward. If there is rock available, Jim has climbed it. Several routes in this book are Jim's creations, and many others have been used by Jim in the course of a mountain day.

Geoff Dewitt deserves particular thanks. After enjoying most of the routes in the first *Scrambles* guide, Geoff and his companions Maurice Tedd and Dick Hogg, embarked on a systematic appraisal of other scrambling possibilities in the Lake District; often running parallel with my own explorations. Geoff's notes and comments have proved an invaluable aid in the production of this guide.

Finally a thank you to my long-standing companions, who I hope enjoyed the days as much as I did: John Riding, Albert Riding, Bill Todd, Gladys Sellers and Aileen Evans.

Brian Evans
January 1990

CONTENTS

FOREWORD

The first volume of *Scrambles in the Lake District* (1982) brought an enthusiastic response. The book was aimed at those with some experience of climbing and mountaineering. It opened the eyes of many people to the adventurous possibilities that exist in the Lake District. Rock climbers found that the scrambles were useful to salvage something out of a poor day, sometimes more than enough to set the adrenalin flowing. Other people found that it changed their concept of a day's fell walking.

This second volume is by no means inferior. Many of the described routes are of excellent quality and rank with the best in the Lake District. There is perhaps a greater emphasis on gills, but these provide entertaining routes to summits, often giving a much greater length of scrambling on clean rock than is available on the crags.

Preparing this volume has given me a host of memorable days, with familiar fells seen in a new light. Even in places I thought I knew intimately a new scramble has revealed different views. The appeal of the details revealed by gill scrambling is intense: the bold form of water sculpted rock with its subtlety of colour: deep green pools and diamond spray cascades.

Many people asked me why such and such a route had not been included in the first volume. On some, like the classic Esk Gorge and Mill Gill, high water had always foiled my attempts. Others I had to 'discover' for myself, often finding signs of previous passage, or even that Victorian mountaineers had enjoyed the same routes. My role is one of compilation and rediscovery of routes that would otherwise lie forgotten. Let those who say the Lake District is overcrowded join the throngs on the popular tourist paths. Scramblers can always find seclusion!

R.Brian Evans
1990

INTRODUCTION

Scrambling as a sport is not new. The ascent of easy rocks where hands may be used is naturally satisfying and has been enjoyed by mountaineers since the sport began. The majority of Alpine peaks involve some scrambling in their ascent by their normal routes. The early rock climbers created routes which involved roped scrambling, without the numerous aids to safety which climbers use today. Many of the Lake District scrambles have been known since Victorian times, many have been used at odd times by generations of climbers. In recent years high standard rock climbing has become so specialized that it is a sport far removed from the rock climbing of even twenty or thirty years ago. Low standard routes are no longer relevant in a climber's guidebook full of Extremes, but it is difficult to know just where to draw the line; where scrambling becomes rock climbing. I consider scrambling to be an ascent of rock where the hands are necessary for progress. Usually the holds are comforting, yet if there is need for a few difficult rock moves in order to overcome an obstacle, then that is acceptable.

Climbers expecting long continuous rock routes may be disappointed. The Lake District scrambles use what the area has to offer and cannot compare with the extensive scrambling available in Skye or other basically craggier areas. Do not expect rock climbs; more a series of rock incidents in a day on the hills. Much is left to the individual - on many of the routes it is a simple matter to bypass most of the rock and reduce the outing to a steep walk. You can often choose to make the route more difficult by seeking steeper rock problems. I have described what I consider to be an interesting line, which if lost need not be a calamity, for you may find an equally worthy way.

Dangers

Scrambling is an adventure sport, which implies that it is dangerous. Part of the attraction of any such sport lies in safely overcoming the potential hazards. Unlike modern rock climbing which is steep and generally well protected, a fall whilst scrambling can be very serious. You must return to the maxim followed by rock climbers before the advent of modern gear -YOU MUST NOT SLIP!

It is appropriate to reiterate some of the comments in *Scrambles in the Lake District*.

'Scrambling is ascending rock that is not usually difficult or steep enough to warrant the term 'rock climbing.' However, a word of warning - although the easier scrambles are quite within the capabilities of a wide range of people - with care - **it is worth remembering that unroped scrambling in exposed situations is potentially the most dangerous of all mountaineering situations.** On the more difficult scrambles the exposure is often dramatic, and it is advisable to take a rope for safety. Persons tackling these should have some experience of rock climbing and the necessary belay and rope techniques to allow a safe ascent or retreat. Good judgement is needed to attempt the routes in bad weather, but an experienced climber will know just how far he can go on wet or greasy rock and **will know when to retreat. Adventurous walkers who are using this book should tackle the easiest routes only in good conditions.** Snow and ice will turn most of the routes into serious and difficult winter climbs. It is inadvisable to venture on them at all in wintry conditions, as verglas over the easiest rocks can create an impossible and dangerous hazard.'

Inevitably there are accidents. Some due to inexperience, some to foolhardiness, some to pure bad luck.

Any adventure sport is hazardous, otherwise it would not be adventurous. The rewards are great, the penalties severe. A recommended book which delves into the philosophy of the subject is Colin Mortlock's *The Adventure Alternative* (Cicerone Press). Mortlock has many thought provoking theories and divides adventure into bands. Every individual has his adventure threshold, the boundary between intense enjoyment and command of the situation, and fear which could result in misadventure. For some individuals that threshold is quite low, others need a much more gripping situation to savour the adventure. Find your threshold and keep within your own limits.

First Aid

Someone in the party should carry a first aid kit to deal with any minor injury. A recommended book is *First Aid for Hillwalkers* by Renouf and Hulse (Cicerone Press). In case of major accidents which require assistance from the Mountain Rescue, go to the nearest telephone, dial 999 and ask for Police.

Notes on Equipment and Technique

Guidance on scrambling technique is not adequately dealt with in most mountaineering text books which tend to concentrate on rock climbing. A recommended read is Steve Ashton's *Hill Walking and Scrambling* (Crowood Press). The following notes are derived from my own experience and are relevant to the particular situations encountered in the Lake District.

EQUIPMENT

A rope <u>must</u> be carried in the party, to be used when the leader deems that the weakest member needs assurance, or when the route is extremely exposed as on an open crag. It is unwise to carry the rope around the shoulders as this impedes vision and tends to snag in dangerous places. Always keep the rope in the rucksack but easily accessible when required.

A scrambling slip is more likely to result in a fall over easy-angled or broken rock than the steep free falls of genuine rock climbing. This is more likely to result in injury than on a steep crag. Assuming that the leader is highly competent and will not fall, the rope is required to stop slips by weaker members of the party. The rope can be 9mm and the longer the better. 40m is a good length and can be used singly or double as occasion demands. It allows a reasonable length for abseiling out of difficulty. In most of the easier gills a shorter safety rope is adequate. A few belay slings and karabiners are necessary. A couple of long tape slings allow trees or spikes to be used as belays. Two or three smaller slings with nuts (rocs) of different sizes complete the gear. There is no need to clutter oneself with the excessive hardware commonly used in modern rock climbing.

Helmets are not usually necessary, although in a large party care must be exercised to avoid knocking stones on those following. If the rope is used, again take care that the rope does not flick any loose stones on those below.

Scrambling is usually done in boots. Best are medium-weight with a semi-stiff sole and narrow welt. There is no need for expensive rigid, mountaineering boots. Some people prefer lightweight boots, which encourage a neat approach. Avoid cheap bendy 'Fell Boots' sold in many non-specialist shops. Choose your boots with care as secure footwear is a vital safety factor. Trainers, with socks over the top, can be useful in certain circumstances, particularly in a greasy gill. The trainers need to be sturdy and well fitting. Avoid old bendy, floppy trainers. Note that trainers are not a substitute for boots, but an additional aid.

Belays
The rope is of little use unless the party can be safely belayed to a firm anchorage. Modern safety techniques are not the prerogative of the climber, and the scrambler must learn the basics. Sometimes trees or spikes can be utilised as anchors, but more often these are lacking and a nut belay must be inserted into a crack of suitable width. To this end a selection of three or four varying sized nuts, slings and karabiners should be carried in the party. One of the slings should be a long tape which can also serve as an abseil sling.

Needless to say, anyone unfamiliar with the techniques required to use the above, must study a basic rock climbing instruction book and thoroughly practice. However, do not be put off - the placement of a firm belay is largely a matter of common sense and the rope handling requirements are quickly learned.

Other Equipment
As most scrambles will be incorporated into a longer walk or combination of scrambles, a rucksack will normally be carried with all that you deem necessary - a compass, torch, lunch, waterproofs and a spare pair of dry socks (to put on after a gill scramble). The best maps are the O.S. 1:25,000 Outdoor Leisure Series, Nos. 4, 5, 6 and 7.

Techniques
The most basic requirement is to ascend rock without either slipping

or pulling the holds away. In the gills slippery rock is a natural hazard, varying according to location. Always expect your foot to slip if placed on a sloping hold - ensure that your handholds are sufficient to regain control. When crossing slippery gill beds place the boot between rocks so that it will tighten its hold if it slips. Use sharp edged footholds, even if they are smaller than more obvious slippery sloping ones. If the pitch is obviously slippery then either take boots off and proceed in socks, or put socks over trainers brought specifically for the purpose. Note that trainers are more bendy than boots and will not be as secure on small holds. Be aware that socks wear through!

Pulling holds away is easier than you may think, particularly in a fault controlled gill where the basic structure may be shattered. If there is any possibility that a flake fingerhold may ping off, use it with caution and delicacy. Spikes may be large but insecure. Treat them with respect. Even on the best rock there are loose holds and perched blocks. Aim to avoid a sudden upset of balance. A heave and pull approach can be positively dangerous, particularly if the person is unaware of the dangers. Do not pull outwards on any hold where there is the possibility that it may become detached. Upward progress can often be made more safely by pushing rather than pulling. Knees can be useful.

Easy-angled waterslides pose few problems to climbers used to balance climbing. Non-climbers tend to reach ever higher for non-existent jug handle holds, which makes a slip more probable as the weight of the body is transferred from a vertical position (which helps to hold the foot in place) to a position almost parallel to the slabs, (which helps to push the foot off the hold). A slip on a waterslide slab can result in a long dangerous slide and people below can be swept off like skittles.

Think twice before taking children on scrambles. Whilst they are often natural scramblers and show little fear, they do not possess experience or sound judgement. They need constant supervision and should be roped at all times. Leave your dog below for the duration of the trip. Whilst it is possible to push and pull a dog up the easiest gills, it is not fair on you or it. If left to run loose, it will run round the hazards often seeking an escape up loose and vegetated side walls, sending rocks down on the party.

To sum up, the safest scrambler is someone with a background of many years experience of mountaineering, who can cope with rock climbing situations, loose or slippery rock, has a cautious approach and is not afraid of deciding that conditions render an expedition unsafe.

Roped Scrambling

In gills a short rope is necessary to safeguard occasional steep or exposed passages. Most of the scrambling will be done unroped.

On buttresses, or craglets, the scrambling is much more open and exposed, route finding is important and it is easy for the inexperienced to push into a situation where ascent is dangerous and retreat frightening. In these situations roped scrambling is the only relatively safe solution, coupled with sound belaying techniques. Unroped scrambling on grade 2 or 3 routes is only for the very experienced climber/scrambler. The longer the rope the better. 40m 9mm is a good compromise. Crag scrambling should only be done in good dry conditions.

Solo Scrambling

Many competent mountaineers enjoy solo scrambling, yet the dangers are many. It is so easy to stray into unforeseen difficulties where retreat is hazardous. In a party, someone can usually bypass the difficulty and drop a rope, alone any mistake could be costly, and a minor incident may become a major problem. Think twice about going alone - it's much more fun with a companion.

Types of Scramble

Most readers of this book will be familiar with the comments expressed in the first volume of *Scrambles in the Lake District*, which basically divides the routes into open crag rock routes or ways which follow gills.

Experienced climbers will find the crags - or craglets - entertaining, where the aim is to seek out a route on as much clean rock as possible, without the technical difficulties of genuine rock climbing. In practice, this often means linking suitable outcrops of rock to form a way up the hillside. Alternatively the route takes a way up ledges and rakes through areas of steeper crag. Obviously this type of scramble is very exposed and failure to find the correct route could be disastrous. Great care is necessary to avoid a slip, and on many routes, (grade 2/3) roped scrambling is the safest means of progression.

Gill scrambling poses few route finding problems, the pitches are often short and there is much less exposure than on crags. The easier gills form a good introduction to scrambling. The Lake District is fortunate in possessing a wealth of gills which give good sport. In years of adventuring in many parts of Europe and Britain I have rarely encountered any counterparts as good as the Lakeland gills.

Gill scrambling demands self imposed rules for maximum enjoyment. Harry Griffin, one of the most enthusiastic of gill scramblers, has described *his* rules in *Adventuring in Lakeland* (Robert Hale). Basically, rule one is to take the hardest route and closest to the water, only straying from the stream bed when the direct way is impassable. Rule two is to stick to the rock as much as possible, only wading - or in extreme cases, swimming - when progress is impossible by climbing. This often means performing difficult rock moves a few inches above a pool, or struggling to ascend a difficulty when it would be much easier to walk round. Griffin advocates a direct approach despite waterfalls and spray and even scorns the idea of doing the gills in drought. I prefer to assume that my legs will get wet but draw the line at anything else, and the gills are described here on that basis. However, water conditions are so variable that each party will probably encounter slightly different problems and have to make their own judgements.

The most serious gill scrambles, some would say the only ones worth doing, lie in ravines, which are common in the Lake District, but having sampled the delights of the clean water-washed rock, more open streams are not to be dismissed. Gills which cascade over broad belts of rock give entertaining scrambling with a choice of route and opportunity to make the ascent as difficult or as easy as you wish. Nevertheless, a rope should be carried to safeguard the occasional hazard and provide protection for anyone in the party who requires it.

Bear in mind that some of the gills are heavily vegetated and can be oppressively luxuriant in the height of summer. Midges can prove troublesome at times.

Conditions

Choosing the right gill for the available conditions needs thought. In a prolonged dry spell go for those special trips which rarely come into perfect condition. These normally carry a good deal of water and drain a large area. The small gills are feasible after a few days of dry weather in summer. In a period of mixed weather the ground remains sodden and you may find more water than you anticipated. A good gill scramble can be rendered useless if you cannot easily criss-cross the stream and utilise water-washed rock.

When Lakeland is blighted by a pall of low-lying unmoving cloud which renders crags slippery and hillwalking unattractive, gills can be entertaining and rewarding, provided there is not too much water flowing. Spring brings other problems. I have been thwarted, on a perfect day in a dry spell, by meltwater.

A dry spell in winter can give good gill scrambling, sheltered from the wind, but beware of ice which lingers in ravines. Water-splashed rock with an almost invisible veneer of ice can be hazardous. In true winter conditions the gills give magnificent winter climbing.

Some concern has been expressed by conservationists and botanists that gill scrambling could lead to the destruction of a sensitive habitat for rare plants. Whilst the passage of people leads to a beaten track, the caring scrambler will appreciate the hanging gardens on the side walls, which remain undisturbed. The best scrambling lies close to the solid water-washed rock and the side walls are used only in emergency as escape routes, so damage to the vegetation should be minimal.

Bad Weather Scrambling

Many rock climbers use scrambles as a means of salvaging something exciting on a poor day. In bad conditions the craglets are treacherously slippery and many a climber has had an epic. Do not underestimate the seriousness of these routes. Remember the aspect of a crag is very important - south and west facing rocks are usually cleaner and quicker drying.

Grading

This is always a tricky subject. It relies so much on the prevailing conditions on the described ascent, although other people's opinions have been taken into account. In the first *Scrambles* some of the routes had their gradings revised, generally upwards, in the light of comments received. In this book many routes are graded 1/2 or 2/3 which indicates that the route can be done at either grade.

Grade 1 is a straightforward scramble, with little or no route finding difficulty. The described route takes the most interesting line, which can usually be varied or even avoided at will. Generally, the exposure is not great, but even so, great care must be taken to avoid a slip.

Grade 2 will contain longer and more difficult stretches of scrambling, where a rope may be found useful for safety in the more exposed passages. Although individual sections of the scramble can usually be avoided, these sections may be inescapable once the scramble is underway. Some skill in route finding is required to follow the described line.

Grade 3 is a more serious proposition, only to be undertaken by competent parties. A rope is advisable for safety on exposed passages and for some pitches which demand easy rock climbing. A steady leader is required, with the ability to judge how the rest of the party are coping with the situations, and a rope should be used wherever the safety of an individual is in doubt.

Grade 3S denotes a particularly serious outing, perhaps containing a very exposed passage on steep rock, poor rock or vegetation. Recommended only for experienced and competent climbers.

Many of the routes are described to follow what I consider to be the most rewarding route for continuity and interest. This often involves the passage of rock outcrops which could be easily avoided by a short detour - thus the grading can be reduced with a consequent loss of interest. So much is up to the choice of the individual. Rock climbers will doubtless choose their own lines to suit their chosen standard.

will doubtless choose their own lines to suit their chosen standard. Rock climbers can use the scrambles as a variation of 'bouldering.'

The star system gives a useful indication of quality. One star represents a route which although not classic, has its good points and is worthy of attention. Two stars represent a route of more continuous interest and a good line, whilst three stars are reserved for classic routes with more continuously interesting scrambling, based on a good line.

Very few of the routes are suitable for descent, as described; but some can be descended close to the described route, by choosing easier alternatives on grassy rakes. Generally, an ascent is so much more worthwhile that it is best to plan an itinerary which combines several ascents, rather than lose interest in an unsatisfactory descent. When looking up a rocky buttress the continuous scrambling is obvious. When looking down, there often appears to be a surfeit of grass and it is difficult to choose a continuous rock descent.

Some of the routes will become easier with use, for the passage of many people leads to cleaner rocks and little paths linking the rock sections, thus reducing route finding.

Exploratory Scrambling

Exploratory scrambling can create some interesting and hazardous days. Most people will be content to tackle the standard good quality routes, but for the person who has done everything - that is, most of the rock climbs and scrambles within his/her grade, and most of the popular summits, scrambling where fancy takes you can be quite satisfying. However, a word of warning - if you are not careful you can easily get into some particularly nasty situations. There is an awful lot of rubbishy crag in the Lake District! The best rough rock lies in the central fells, whilst east of Thirlmere it tends to be smoother and more vegetated. The Skiddaw Slates which comprise all the fells north of Buttermere, except the head of Newlands, are shattered and rarely give good scrambling. One or two gills that seem promising prove slippery and the water-washed channel is usually veiled with a curtain of moss. Some are good winter ice climbs, such as Moss Force and Whitewater Dash, but are of no interest to the scrambler.

The pioneer rock climbers often chose gullies for their climbs, with a mistaken sense of security. I would strongly advise the scrambler to keep away from most gullies, for they are dank and desperate. Invariably the rock is slippery and even the most innocent looking cleft has its bed blocked by chockstones which are often strenuous and serious obstacles.

Stick to the easy-angled little craglets and string them together to make an interesting ascent, or choose a pleasant open stream bed to follow to the tops.

The Routes
The scrambles are described valley by valley beginning with Langdale and then travelling round the area in a clockwise direction to end in the east.

The map reference refers to the approximate start of each route. Right and left means in the direction of travel.

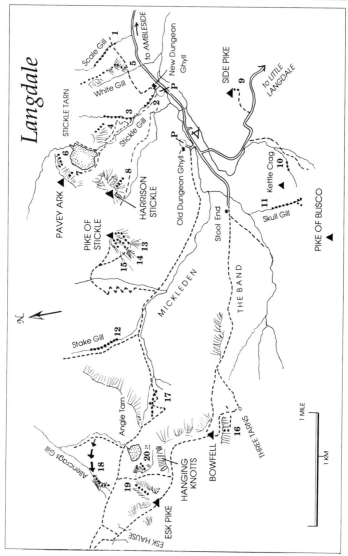

Langdale

Langdale

One of Lakeland's most popular and easily accessible valleys, Langdale is fortunate in possessing a wealth of good scrambling. There are gills to explore, classic rakes, buttresses and ridges with many possibilities for combinations of scrambles which provide ascents mainly on rock for a good part of a mountain day. The routes often culminate on or very close to a summit.

Much of the best rock faces to south or west, which gives quick drying clean rock of excellent quality. A feature of Langdale is rock with a surfeit of good holds and rugosities. Friction is generally good. The routes described fill in several important gaps in the original *Scrambles*, especially the impressive classic route up the front of Pike of Stickle, a serious mountaineering route.

There are campsites at Baysbrown near Chapel Stile, and the popular National Trust site close to the Old Dungeon Ghyll Hotel.

1. SCALE GILL   Grade 1 or 2*   NY 303067

This is the gill on the southern slopes of Blea Rigg and immediately behind the FRCC Raw Head hut and the Achille Ratti hut. It is used for water supplies so care must be taken to avoid pollution.

Approach: For those staying at the climbing huts, approach is simple. Others will do better to park at the official car park near the New Dungeon Ghyll. This has the advantage of being handy for a return down the Stickle Gill path.

From the main car park start by the Stickle Gill path, but leave it almost immediately to go right across a footbridge, then follow the sign 'to White Gill Crag.' up a paved track. Branch right through a gate and along a path above the intake wall. Cross the foot of White Gill, continue below Scout Crag and round the fell shoulder to reach Scale Gill. The path crosses the gill above a steep rocky section which provides good scrambling and should not be missed.

Character: A shallow gill in a narrow fault-controlled ravine. The scrambling is nowhere serious and any difficulties can be avoided. The stream is small and is a mere trickle in a dry spell. Rock is generally good.

The Route: Descend from the path to enter the rocky watercourse. Above the path the stream bed provides a mix of walking and easy scrambling. Where the ravine narrows, the scrambling becomes more continuous and awkward in places. Often there is a 'chicken run' for the more cautious on the left of the stream runnel. The final part of the gill lies up a narrow slit which is easier than it appears - apart from the final chockstone which can be avoided just below on the right.

Emerge onto the broad ridge of Blea Crag. It is a short walk to reach Stickle Tarn and more scrambling on Pavey Ark or Harrison Stickle.

2. STICKLE (MILL) GILL

The scramble was described in the parent guide as starting well above the footbridge. In low water, the gill bed can be followed almost from the start, amongst the trees. There are some interesting little ascents and pools to traverse on good clean rock. (Grade 1)

3. TARN CRAG GILL   Grade 2*   NY 292069

This gill is an insignificant narrow stream which runs right of Tarn Crag. In the 1950's, when climbing on Tarn Crag was quite popular, it provided a well-used approach to the crag.

Approach: From the car park near the New Dungeon Ghyll Hotel, take the well marked path up the side of Stickle Gill, cross the footbridge and continue to a sheepfold just over the stile. The gill is directly above - a narrow tree-lined defile on the right.

Character: Better than it looks, the scrambling is on good rock and the interest is maintained for a considerable way. If difficulties are avoided the grade is reduced to 1.

The Route: The scrambling starts at the base of a cleft. If the water is too high the first fall can be passed on the right, traverse back to enter the cleft. The next fall is passed by bridging until ledges on the right wall can be used to reach the top of the fall. Three easier steps follow to a dark recess which is passed by rocks on the right. The next pitch is a steep fall which is climbed athletically by bulging rocks on the left wall, easier than it looks, with aid from a handy tree root. Regain the stream and continue up a series of steps to where the stream splits. The right branch is best, or the rocks between, to regain better scrambling in the clean stream bed above. There are numerous waterslides and short steep walls to surmount. Here and there a pool traverse demands care.

A more definite ravine is met, guarded at the entrance by a square block. This ravine is more mossy and contains several quite tricky pitches, one especially awkward which can be avoided on the right. Eventually the scrambling peters out.

The rocks of Tarn Crag lie to the left and the following continuation makes a pleasant extension to the scrambling. Alternatively there is a small path on the left of the stream, which leads to the ridge. The lower part of this path has been renovated, a credit to the recent Lakeland pathbuilders. The new path uses the old pony track by the gill to half-height then branches left under Tarn Crag to Stickle Tarn.

4. TARN CRAG - WEST RIB   Grade 2*   NY 292073

This is the continuous rock on the right end of the crags and makes the logical scrambling continuation to the gill.

Approach: From the gill cross bracken slopes to the skyline rib. Start below a steep recess which contains a holly tree.

Character: Typical Langdale rock - solid and knobbly. Exposed in places.

The Route: Start up the rib which runs right of the recess. After 40ft it fizzles out. Traverse left along an exposed shelf above the recess. At its end climb the knobbly slabs. Pass an overhang on the right and

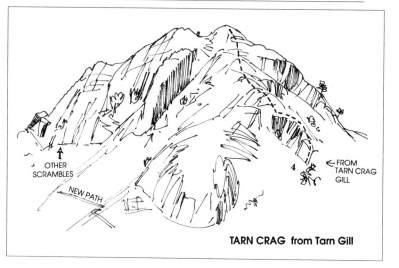

TARN CRAG from Tarn Gill

return to the rib which gives fine scrambling up a succession of slabs, ribs and grooves.

Stickle Tarn and Pavey Ark lie a stroll away.

5. WHITE GHYLL EDGE   Grade 2   NY 297068

A scramble which follows the steep spur which bounds White Ghyll, and incorporates some easy rocks on Scout Crag.

Approach: From the NT car park at the New Dungeon Ghyll, start up the Stickle Ghyll track but almost immediately go right through a gate and cross the stream at a footbridge. Turn left signed White Ghyll Crag, up a paved track. Branch right through a gate and along the top edge of the intake wall, through a wood to cross the normally dry bed of White Ghyll. A few yards further at the highest point of the path, ascend to the left end of the overhanging rock barrier just above. This is Middle Scout Crag.

Character: Good rock but disjointed scrambling with steep walking up bracken slopes between the outcrops. There is scope for climber scramblers to make a more direct ascent of Scout Crag but the route is described in its easiest form. The rock needs to be sought to get the best out of this route otherwise it degenerates into mainly walking.

Route: Start at the extreme left end of the lower rocks. After 20ft move right onto a block and mount a rough staircase to a slabby rib on the right of a tree.

The main rocks of Scout Crag lie across a stony gully on the right. Cross the gully head and descend about 50ft to the foot of the climbers' descent route. This is a stony shelf on the right of a smooth rock buttress. Climb a steep crack for 20ft to the start of the shelf which soon develops into a walk to the head of the right-hand rocks. As soon as possible go left along ledges to reach the left edge of the rocks which give exposed scrambling to the top of the first knoll.

Climb a slabby rib on the left, then go left again to the next outcrop, where a mossy slab slants diagonally right. Keep close to its edge and take care with the rock. The rough rocks ahead end at a knoll where the edge of White Ghyll crags are seen on the left, with a broad rock barrier across the spur above. Reach this barrier by incorporating several tiny craglets on the way, a couple on the left then one on the right.

Right of an overhung recess in the steep wall is a slab glacis which slants R to L. This is the route, across the higher of two shelves to a grass ledge on the left. Move back right to the most continuous rock and up a groove left of a small block.

The outcrops above are scattered and of excellent easy-angled rock. Seek out the most continuous way to the top.

Walk above the top of White Ghyll then left into a shallow combe with a low col at its top overlooking Stickle Tarn. The scrambles on Pavey Ark or Harrison Stickle are close by.

6. PAVEY FAR EAST   Grade 2*   NY 288081

A rambling route which finds some good rock pitches and gives close-up views of the spectacular rock climbs on Pavey's East Wall.

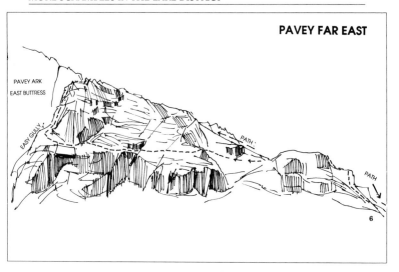

PAVEY FAR EAST

Approach: A path crosses Bright Beck, the north-west inlet of Stickle Tarn and goes right of an overhanging rock outcrop, the furthest rocks on this side of Pavey Ark.

Character: Some interesting pitches, some exposed sheep track, and some of the peculiar knobbly slabs which characterize Pavey. Exposed.

Route: Start on the left of the path below the left end of an overhanging outcrop a short way above the stream. Climb slabs slightly left then move right to pass the left end of the overhang. Go up a bit then climb the steep rocks above by the easiest line; a tricky exposed pitch of rock climbing. Climb the slabs above towards the right - good holds and strange circular markings in the rock.

That completes the first rock outcrop and the scramble seems to have fizzled out. However, a walk left almost horizontally picks up a faint sheep track which passes below a steep little wall and the base of a slab. Continue at the same level, across two patches of bare rock above a steep drop. Go up a little and follow the narrowing bilberry ledge across more slabs to an airy descent of an exposed groove for 10ft to reach a shelf round the corner. This is an excellent viewing platform especially if climbers are tackling the steep routes of Pavey's East Buttress. Zig-zag up right to gain a fine knobbly slab which leads back left towards the edge overlooking Easy Gully. Climb the steep wall above on its right then walk left to the edge again. The block above is climbed rightwards by a series of shelves which develop into a rib.

Finally, cross a roof-like edge with hands on top and feet on the slab, to join the path at the top of Easy Gully.

7. CRESCENT CLIMB - PAVEY ARK   Grade 3s***   NY 285078

This route, first ascended by Fred Botterill and W.E.Palmer in 1907, is a borderline case between scrambling and genuine rock climbing. It is certainly no place for the solo scrambler and <u>must</u> be done roped.

Approach: Paths on either side of Stickle Tarn rise to the foot of Jack's Rake. Just below the Rake a smaller path rises left to a terrace which runs below the crags. Pass below a broad steep wall of slabs to an

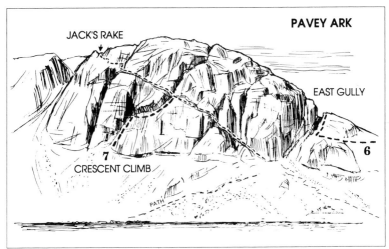

easier angled rib at its left end, just before the steep vegetated Stony Buttress.

Character: Technically the climbing is 'Moderate,' which comes well within the scope of scrambling. Many of the routes described in this book have short sections which are far more difficult, but on Crescent Climb you can't walk round a section you don't like; and once embarked upon the route retreat is a serious undertaking. It must be done as a rock climb, with belays and a sound leader. The atmosphere of the route is that of a big crag - surrounded by steep rock, dripping walls and no alternative easier ways. Imagine the impression it must have made on the pioneers, with their hemp rope and nailed boots - and no belay tapes or nuts. The rock is good on the well-marked route, but some of the flakes should be treated with caution. Several tape slings are useful.

The Route: (1) Follow the cleanest rocks of the rib, which rises in steps. There are a few places where slings can be draped over flakes, but the exposure mounts as height is gained to reach a platform at 140ft. There is a flattish topped spike safe for a down-pull belay and a crack on the right which will accommodate a better nut belay. The line of the traverse below the overhangs above appears very intimidating from here.
(2) 40ft. Continue up the vegetated rib to the left edge of the over-hangs. Slither down to a small ledge with a fine flake belay, on the edge of an impressive void.
(3) 50ft. Traverse across the airy slabs below the overhangs, on comforting handholds and good footholds. The slabs stay wet after rain. It soon eases onto a grass rake. Belay at the far end.
(4) 80ft. Easy scrambling up slabs to a tree belay just below Jack's Rake.

Climbers taking a trip into history will take the logical continuation of GWYNNE'S CHIMNEY (Difficult), the start of which lies a short way down Jack's Rake. This was first ascended in 1892 and is technically more difficult than the Crescent. It is steeper, more strenuous and stays greasy after wet weather. Nevertheless it provides an entertaining route of two pitches, with more scrambling above to the summit.

8. HARRISON STICKLE - SOUTH CENTRAL BUTTRESS
Grade 3** NY 283072

Harrison Stickle is a scrambler's peak with infinite choice. This route accepts the challenge of the steepest buttress.

Approach: From the path between Pike How and the upper part of Dungeon Gill, the buttress is directly below the summit and lies to the left of a deep gully. Scramble up introductory rocks to white slabs at the base of the buttress.

Character: A climber's scramble which passes fairly easily up steep rocks. Exposed rock climbing situations on perfect rock. Rope recommended.

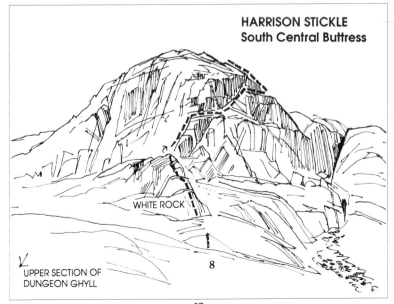

HARRISON STICKLE
South Central Buttress

WHITE ROCK

8

UPPER SECTION OF
DUNGEON GHYLL

The Route: Climb the subsidiary light rocks. Above is a more compact triangular chunk of rock, light coloured at its base. Climb the right-hand rib of this. Where the colour changes, it steepens and is best climbed 15ft left of the right end.

From the top of the pyramid a groove slants right through steep rock for 70ft to a bilberry ledge. Ignore the tempting rocks above which soon steepen, so traverse the ledge right and it becomes a diagonally rising groove. Where it merges into steeper rock step round a block and traverse a horizontal ledge right to easy rocks overlooking the gully. Come back left onto the slabs of the buttress front to finish satisfyingly at the mountain summit.

9. SIDE PIKE, SOUTH RIDGE   Grade 1   NY 293052

The pert little peaklet of Side Pike (1,187ft) on the south side of Langdale, is a popular evening stroll, or time filler, for its ascent takes little more than half an hour and the view is panoramic. The ascent described adds just a little adventure to the trip.

Approach: About ¹/4 mile along the Blea Tarn road from the summit of the pass, at a cattle-grid on the Little Langdale side, a path strikes steeply towards the summit. Where the path veers to the left take to the lowest rocks of the ridge on the right.

The Route: The ridge is the easy-angled rock spur which runs directly to the summit. At first there is some vegetation to avoid. Cross a path (which leads to the rock climbs on the short steep right wall of the upper part of the ridge). Continue on sound clean rock. At a grass ledge the easiest way lies to the right. Finish the scramble by surmounting a prominent block. Descend by the main path along the summit ridge, to the top of the Blea Tarn road.

10. REDACRE GILL   Grade 2   NY 283048

Little scrambling, but worth incorporating in passing for the waterfall pitch.

Approach: The track by Redacre Gill from Wall End is the most popular walkers' route up Pike o'Blisco. The ravine with the water-fall is hidden behind a spur of Kettle Crag. Traverse into the bed of the ravine from the path.

Character: Mossy, but good solid rock well endowed with positive holds. Best after a few days of dry weather when the lower fall can be climbed direct.

The Route: Approach by mild scrambling up the stream bed to an amphitheatre of crag. The main stream cascades directly ahead. If the conditions allow, climb the fall direct to a damp mossy recess, which can also be reached by a zig-zag route on the left. The upper fall is climbed on its left. Where the going gets tough a tree root proves welcome.

11. SKULL GILL   Grade 1 (or 2 by the stream finish)   NY 051276
This is the steep, straight, verdant ravine which lies west of Kettle Crag.

Approach: Take the Oxendale track from Stool End until past the wall and the stream can be crossed to gain the foot of the ravine which cuts deeply into the side of the fall.

Character: An almost dead-straight course in a steep walled cleft, worth a visit for its oppressive atmosphere. The upper part is quite verdant, possibly best saved for a windy winter day when it could prove sheltered and mildly exciting. There is very little genuine scrambling, mainly bouldery walking, unless the stream finish is taken.

The Route: The way is obvious with a couple of easy pitches climbed on the right. Where two streams converge take the left branch. Continue up the bed to where the stream enters over the right wall. The easy escape continues up the now dry bed of the gill.

Stream Finish *(approx. 100ft):* A more sporting climax is to ascend the steep right wall by clean holds amongst the moss-covered rock. Emerge right onto an easier angled sweep of water-washed rock which leads to below a vertical headwall down which the stream dribbles. Escape to the right onto the open fell.

If continuing to the summit of Pike o'Blisco, several rock tiers can be incorporated along the way. If descending to the valley, traverse the hillside left above the ravines to the saddle by Kettle Crag. Keep to the right of the stream to join the well trodden path by Redacre Gill.

12. STAKE GILL   Grade 1 or 2**   NY 260077
Stake Gill borders the Stake Pass path at the head of Langdale. It is well worth visiting for its own sake and can be combined with routes on Pike of Stickle. The upper part of the gill is continuously interesting.

Approach: From the car park at the Old Dungeon Ghyll, go round the back of the hotel and continue along the flat valley base of Mickleden to the head of the valley where Stake Gill is seen on the right. Leave the Stake path past a clump of trees, above a dead tree in the gill and traverse to the foot of the first waterslide.

Character: A combination of good clean, rough, solid rock and interesting scrambling make this a pleasant trip. Whilst it is best visited when the flow is low, the width of rock makes some scrambling possible even in relatively high water. Any difficulties are easily avoided.

The Route: The waterslide slab makes a fine start to the route and is followed by another easier slide. The stream bends in a rock defile. Either scramble easily with the main stream or take the more difficult steep little overflow channel to its left. The gill narrows. After a tricky start on the steep left wall, straddle the flow to reach easier ground. A more serious hazard is presented by a small waterchute around a capstone at the head of a pool. If there is too much water, escape from

Stake Gill

the gill lower down on the right. If the water is low you may still get sprayed as you pass the lip. More cascades provide good scrambling to an overhung recess. The direct route just left of the flow is possible in low water, otherwise avoid by going further left. Broad slabs continue and just when you think all is over there is another little defile to finish.

For Pike of Stickle, branch right on a small path just as the drumlin filled hollow is entered.

PIKE OF STICKLE

The profile of Pike of Stickle must be one of the most photographed views in the Lake District, its bold rocky front extending almost a thousand feet from its blunt summit to the screes of Stickle Breast. There are no rock climbs of any consequence on this extensive face, for the crags are rarely steep or continuous, yet its challenge to a scrambler are obvious. There are numerous possibilities, from the short West Ridge described in the previous guide, to a full frontal attack. Right of the West Ridge is a longer buttress to the left of a deep

PIKE O'STICKLE from Bowfell

gully and right again is the main face, guarded at two-thirds height by a steep band of grey rock. The dauntingly steep direct approach can be avoided by traversing in from the north-west above Traughton Beck, or a scramble up Stake Gill.

Any scramble on Pike of Stickle is an adventure for the experienced, an exposed mountaineering route reminiscent of route finding on Alpine peaks, with the attraction of ending on a summit. In the lower part of the face there is a lot of vegetation, which diminishes as height is gained. The upper part of the mountain gives excellent exposed scrambling. There are some poised blocks to be aware of, although the basic rock is solid and well supplied with holds. In wet conditions the rock becomes slippery. To be completely safe, scram-

Long Crag, Coniston. Long, easy, rough textured slabs give pleasant scrambling. Aileen Evans and Albert Riding.

Shudderstone How, Seathwaite, Duddon Valley. Gladys Sellers on a delicate slab. The route begins at the outcrop by the lake.

Cowcove Beck, Eskdale. Aileen Evans traverses a deep pool, encouraged by John Riding.

Crook Crag, Eskdale. The Great Whinscale route gives excellent scrambling on perfect rock.

bling here should be done roped. Belays are not always easy to find as many of the obvious spikes are unsound and others are flat-topped. All in all, the routes demand an experienced competent leader.

13. PIKE OF STICKLE - MAIN FACE   Grade 2***   NY 273073
A route which takes the easiest way up the broad frontal main face of the mountain, bypassing the Grey Band where it dwindles into insignificance at its right end. Whilst the scrambling is not difficult if the described route is followed, the situation is very exposed and a rope should be used for safety in the upper section.

Approach: From the ODG car park, take the path up the valley bottom until past the base of Pike of Stickle. A zig-zag path mounts the steep spur on the left of Traughton Gill to emerge on a flat moor. The crags of Pike of Stickle are in profile on the right. We are aiming for a platform above the lowest rocks. From Traughton Gill the path rises to a grass shelf. Leave the main path here and follow the shelf right, where a descending sheep track leads into and crosses the steep scree gully to reach a terrace on the crag face. Continue along the terrace to a deep grassy gully where the route starts.

Character: See general comments on Pike of Stickle. The first part of the route ascends the grassy gully in order to break through the first band of steep, vegetated rocks which are of no interest to the scrambler. Once the good rock is reached on the upper part of the peak, the scramble becomes excellent and ends satisfyingly on the mountain summit.

The Route: Start up the gully, which proves to be slightly better than it looks. The way lies directly up the narrow rock bed, almost hidden in places by vegetation, and with the occasional steep step. Avoid a mossy wall by a small detour right and back into the gully to enter an amphitheatre with a slabby right wall, after about 200ft.
    Continue up the gully bed to join a track which enters from the left. Follow this track up right on a broad heather slope to the foot of the

main rocks at some prominent dark cracks in a steep wall.

At this point the rock scrambling begins in earnest. The steep wall is climbed at the prow about 20ft right of the cracks. Zig-zag first right then left to reach a terrace at the top of the cracks. Go up left to another grass terrace. The rocks above are inviting but lead into difficult rock, so walk along the grass terrace a few feet right to a break in the wall. There is a slabby recess with an overhang. Climb the slabs and go left round the overhang to reach a groove, exit left and continue to belay at a table rock below the Grey Band.

Walk about 50ft right below the steep rocks, mount a perched block and the steep step above. We are now level with the top of the steep Grey Band. Continue in the same line, about 60ft, along the break until just past a cleft, where it is feasible to traverse left across slabs onto the front of the buttress. Go diagonally leftwards by a line of small flakes to a ledge and leaning block.

Just right of the block, climb up a few feet to reach a line of rightward leading shelves which lead across the face onto easier angled slabs and the summit.

14. THE GREY BAND ROUTE   3S and Very Difficult**
NY 273073

This route takes the challenge of the left side of the main face, just right of the deep gully in the upper half of the crag. The Grey Band is steep and is crossed by a pitch of genuine rock climbing in an exposed situation. Rope essential.

Character: A serious mountaineering route with a mixture of scrambling and rock climbing. The Grey Band is a steep obstacle. Only for experienced climber/scramblers.

Approach: As for the Main Face but before the starting gully of that route ascend steep grass to avoid the first steep rock outcrop.

The Route: Start in the centre of a low rock wall directly below a prominent dark crack in the tier above. The route is described in pitches.

(1) There is a shallow mossy groove with cleaner rocks on its left. Go

diagonally left with a delicate exit onto a grass terrace. Belay 15ft left of the obvious dark mossy crack.

2) Go leftwards up a break to the foot of a clean slab. Continue diagonally left onto easy ground on the right of a gully. Belay spike in centre of rock wall.

(3) Semi-circle right on a rock staircase to a shelf below a prominent chimney cleft formed by a huge poised block. Scramble to the foot of this and nut belay on block on left.

(4) Go round the right side of the huge block and climb a flake at its back onto a juniper ledge. Exit from the ledge at the left end, awkwardly, to reach a juniper terrace at the foot of the Grey Band. Nut belay in thin crack just on right.

(5) This pitch involves rock climbing of about V.Diff standard with no easier alternatives. Walk along the terrace for 30ft to a break in the forbidding wall. Ascend bilberry ledges leftwards, then cross a rib to gain a corner on the left, which makes a steep finish. Spike belay above on right.

(6) Easier ground rightwards.

(7) Continue rightwards past smoother slabs to a break back left. Belay behind huge block.

(8) Leftwards again to another terrace.

(9) Continue to the summit.

15. PIKE OF STICKLE - WEST GULLY RIBS   Grade 2*
NY 273074

Between the West Gully and the West Ridge are two rocky ribs. This scramble seeks the best combination.

Approach: The route can be reached from above and is useful as an ideal filler after the main fare. From the col on the Stake side of the summit rock pyramid, descend the steep slopes to cross scree to the foot of the West Ridge. Continue the descent on the spur then traverse to the base of the slabs at the start of the scramble.

Character: Not so continuous as the other routes here, but the excellent rock on the upper narrow rib makes it worthwhile. Exposed in places.

The Route: Climb the broad band of slabs on the left of the deep cut gully, to a terrace. Continue up a series of grassy ledges overlooking the gully. Avoid a steeper wall by moving into the gully. At the level of a chockstone regain the buttress front and go well left on a grass ledge below a steep wall, to reach another rib left of a shallow gully.

Climb the rib at its right edge on good rock to a platform. A steep step right across the wall leads into an easier groove round the corner. Climb slabs up the rib front then move right onto a rock staircase. The narrow rib continues with interest to a narrow neck at the top of the gully, where a path is joined. Spurn the path and continue up the rocks above to the summit.

16. BOWFELL LINKS - PINNACLE RIB   Grade 1*   NY 245063

Above the col of Three Tarns, on the south side of Bowfell are the crags of The Links. A row of buttresses offers considerable scope for scrambling on quite good rock, with some loose lying blocks. The right-hand buttresses are narrow and steep in parts. Any scrambling here is verging on genuine rock climbing. In the middle, the angle is easier and the described route takes this, possibly the easiest buttress on the crag. Further left the crags become more broken and capped by a steeper tower, but the scrambling is disjointed, with many loose blocks.

Approach: Nearest parking is the Old Dungeon Ghyll Hotel in Langdale, whence a lane leads to Stool End and the path up The Band. Bear left at its top to reach Three Tarns. Cross toilsome screes to the foot of the crags and pass below four gullies to reach a prominent pinnacle at the foot of a ridge.

Character: A short, open scramble on rough rocks, care required in places with loose blocks. Pleasant enough, with a crag atmosphere.

The Route: Climb the front of the pinnacle and move right into the gap. (It is quite tricky to ascend to the top and the descent has an awkward

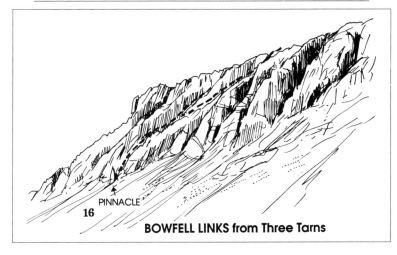

PINNACLE

16

BOWFELL LINKS from Three Tarns

step.) Behind the pinnacle continue on a solid sweep of light coloured slabs interspersed with ledges.

The rock changes to grey, but is still good quality. Keep to the left edge overlooking a shallow scree gully. Where the rib merges into the gully cross to the rib on the right. This gives good scrambling past a steep little wall, (which can be turned on the right). An easier angled rock spine emerges on a shelf with the summit ahead and the path a few yards to the right.

The rest of Bowfell is disappointing for scramblers - there are no worthwhile possibilities above the Climbers' Traverse towards Bowfell Buttress, although the path is very scenic as it traverses below the steep walls of Flat Crags and then ascends the screes on the side of the Great Slab. The Slab is not worth investigating, for although the angle is easy, it is mossy and slippery.

Hanging Knotts on the north side of the mountain, overlooking Angle Tarn is impressive and appears worthy of scrambling, but the rock is quite steep, despite being broken by ledges, and is very slippery in anything less than bone dry conditions.

The following scrambles are described together as they form an interesting excursion.

17. ROSSETT SLABS   Grade 1   NY 252073

The walk up Rossett Gill footpath, at the head of Langdale, can be enlivened by a little sport up the rocks at its side. Good rough rock. Where the path begins to rise after it crosses the stony base of Rossett Gill, the path swings left to the base of slabs. These make pleasant scrambling. Where the first crag band peters out move right onto more slabs and regain the path at the top of a knoll. The next crags are broken, so follow the path on a long zig-zag left and back right to reach another continuous belt of slabs on the right. A prominent clean crag above the path is too steep for scrambling but could provide a climbing pitch.

Join the path at the head of Rossett Gill and continue to Angle Tarn.

18. ALLEN CRAGS GILL   Grade 1*   NY 243084

Although strictly speaking this belongs to Langstrath and Borrowdale it is most conveniently approached from Langdale.

Approach: At the outlet of Angle Tarn follow the path right down by the stream. The popular Esk Hause path is soon left behind as you enter the lonely head of Langstrath. Either drop down to the valley floor and take a cairned but almost untrodden path up the side of Allen Crags Gill, or contour the steep slopes to reach the gill. The scrambling starts well up the gill, in a steep walled straight-cut ravine.

The Route: The ravine is bouldery to a junction where the main stream enters from the left over slabs. Climb the rocks just left of the watercourse to a cascade in the bed of a groove with fine slabs on its left. Either zig-zag easily about 20ft left of the groove or climb the slabs direct. Continue close to the stream up another slab into a recess where the stream splits into two channels, the left easier and less mossy. After another slab the angle eases where the ravine becomes more square-cut. Climb a rib in the centre, pass a fallen block and climb a rib on the left. Pass through a narrows, in the water flow and finish up a broad rock band.

Join the main Esk Hause footpath. For a continuation scramble on Esk Pike at a similar grade, go left to the highest point of the path before it descends to Angle Tarn. At right angles is a broad spur which drops from the flat top of Esk Pike. This forms the route.

19. ESK PIKE - NORTH WEST SPUR   Grade 2 in places
NY 240077

Approach: From Rossett Gill overlooking Angle Tarn, the rocks are obvious beyond the path to Ore Gap, or approach as described from Allen Crags Gill.

Character: Good quality rough rock on a broad spur. The best route needs to be sought to avoid easy ground, but some of the situations feel quite airy.

The Route: There is a subsidiary knot of compact rock below the main slabs, about 100ft right of the path. Start at the lowest left rib. Climb slabs left of a mossy streak to pass an overlap on its right. Above is a recess. Move left 10ft to ascend a steep awkward V-groove (Grade 2). Finish over a rock fin.

The main slabs lie ahead, the nearest rocks on the right. Climb these left of a mossy streak. Pass a steepening on the right and reach a grass terrace. Continue ahead up a broad broken rib where easy ground lies just to the right. Go left to better rocks across a grassy gully. The side wall of the gully is steep - step onto a sharp flake to gain a ledge. Traverse this descending slightly to round the corner left and up a rib. Pass a bulge on the left, then back right. Easier slabs and broken ground to a recess, passed by the slab on the right of an overhang. The rib above soon curls into walking and the summit ridge of Esk Pike lies not far ahead.

20. HANGING KNOTTS GILL   Grade 3   NY 243076

This is a narrow stream which drops into Angle Tarn on the right-hand side of Hanging Knotts. It is only worth considering when the stream is virtually dry, as the rock bed is narrow and mossy.

Approach: From Langdale by the Rossett Gill path to Angle Tarn or by the scramble on the Rossett Slabs.

Character: Steep and serious where it cuts through a band of crag.

The Route: There is a square-cut break through the first crag. Climb the steep cascade left or right. The cascade above is climbed close to the water flow by mossy steps to a ledge. A steep awkward spout to the left is quite exposed. The final narrowing poses another steep awkward pitch. Finish on the vertical right wall.

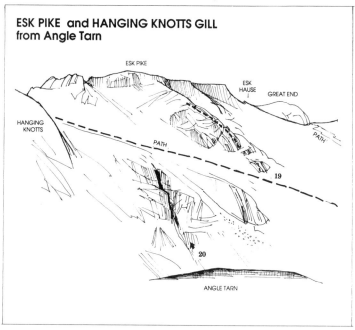

ESK PIKE and HANGING KNOTTS GILL from Angle Tarn

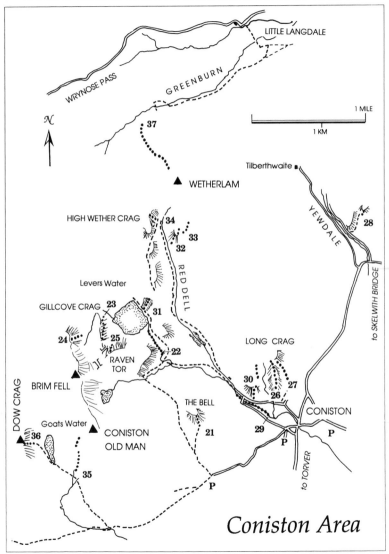

Coniston Area

The entire eastern flank of the Coniston Fells offers much good scrambling on rock which is usually very rough textured and furnished with holds. There are numerous rocky outcrops which can be strung together to make an entertaining and logical progression. Whilst some of the routes are short and hardly justify a star grade individually, they can provide a very satisfying combination.

The area is one of the most popular in the Lake District, yet even here the scrambler will penetrate quieter corners away from the crowds.

Do not be tempted into exploring the open holes and clefts of old mine workings in this area, for they have false floors, held only by rotting timbers and the hidden chasms may descend hundreds of feet.

There are campsites at Torver and along the edge of Coniston Water.

21. THE BELL   Grade 1*   SD 977288

This tiny peaklet makes a fine start to a day's scrambling. The route takes an obvious frontal rock rib.

Approach: Park just beyond the fell gate of the Walna Scar road and take the quarry road right. The Bell is the prominent rocky knoll on the right. 200 yards along the road, at Braidy Beck, take a green path right which passes Bell Cottage. Keep close to a wall to cross a stream and then force a way leftwards through bracken to the foot of the rocks.

Character: Nice rock, good holds, a pity the route is so short.

The Route: As you approach the rocky pyramid there is a prominent slabby ridge directly facing. Start at a little flaky ridge of 50ft, then move left to the slabby rocks. Follow a left slanting ramp past a juniper onto the front of the slabs and up to a grass terrace.

THE BELL 21

The slabby wall above is climbed direct for 20ft to a ledge, then move right and up to a grass ledge. Escape right again to an edge. Continue up the ridge direct, or more easily just on its left. There is a horizontal terrace with a prominent tree on the right. Scramble up the back of a recess, to the left of the tree, to reach easy-angled rocks. (At the terrace, you could walk left to gain a more continuous sweep of rock.) Finally mount rough green slabs to the summit spine.

From the top of the knoll, an undulating craggy ridge leads to the quarry road close to where it turns left and heads steeply uphill. The path to the Pudding Stone and Levers Water branches right here.

A logical continuation of easy scrambling is to continue up Levers Water Beck.

22. LEVERS WATER BECK   Grade 1   SD 283988

The stream which descends from Levers Water drops over several rock steps which provide an interesting way of gaining height although the scramble is scrappy.

Approach: The most straightforward approach is from the Coppermines Valley, by the mine track past the old workings of Paddy End. The rough track crosses the stream by a bridge below Grey Crag.

If you are approaching from the Walna Scar road and the preceding scramble, take the path right from the quarry road, to the Pudding Stone, which makes an interesting ascent if you so wish. Cross the stream beyond and branch right immediately on an old track which runs below Grey Crag to the bridge over Levers Water Beck.

Character: A rather disjointed route but the individual rock steps are quite good.

The Route: From the bridge gain the stream bed and dependent on water level use the rocks as much as possible. An old incline bounds the stream on the left. The first two rock steps are most easily ascended on the left, the third is steeper and is ascended on the right of the stream. Note the old metal spikes in the stream bed, for this is where the mine track crossed. Start this rock step about 30ft right of the stream. Good holds trend leftwards to a ledge below smoother rocks. Move left to mount steeply close to the water in a fine position, on comforting holds.

The final hazard is a wall of crag with a waterfall at its right edge. The easiest way is by a groove on the left edge of the crag, which is ascended to a capstone. Escape right or crawl under. The dam of Levers Water lies just ahead.

A more difficult alternative (Grade 3) is to traverse the left wall until near the waterfall where a steep climb is made first left then direct.

On the last part of the ascent you will have noticed a dark hole in the crags above to the left. This is Simon's Nick, a notorious feature of the mining legacy. From the top of the last fall on the beck scramble, a path leads down left and gives access to the foot of the Nick, across some ochre screes.

Do not be tempted into exploring the open holes and clefts in this area, for they have false floors, held only by rotting timbers and the

hidden chasms may descend hundreds of feet.

23. GILLCOVE CRAG - NORTH EDGE   Grade 2   SD 275994

Gillcove Crag is a broad swathe of rock and vegetation overlooking Levers Water. Its north-easterly aspect ensures a liberal coating of lichen and slow drying rock. A grade 3 scramble is reported on the left-hand rib, with a nice delicate traverse, but the route described is more in-keeping with other scrambles in the area.

Approach: Either walk up the Coppermines Valley from Coniston to Levers Water, or use the shorter approach from the car parking at the fell gate of the Walna Scar Track, via the Pudding Stone and Boulder Valley, from where a path straight ahead leads to a tiny col left of Simon's Nick overlooking Levers Water. A track about 100 feet above the lake skirts below the crags to reach Cove Beck. The right-hand edge of the crags lies just left of the stream.

Character: The rock is rather smooth, lies generally in shadow and stays slippery after rain, yet is of good quality. Care is required. The scramble takes a series of rock walls along the right edge of the crags.

The Route: Start at the first lowest rocks left of Cove Beck, but the easiest way lies about 20ft up the right-hand side. After about 40ft move left along grass to gain a rib by a delicate step, and mount to a large terrace. Continue straight ahead to another terrace. Go left a few yards to reach knobbly slabs just left of a rib and climb slabs to another terrace.

   The next buttress drops away to the left. On its face opposite are two grass ledges below a skyline block. The first grass ledge (identified by a quartz slab) is gained by a steep ascent on good holds at its right end. Go left and climb easily to the second ledge. Slabs continue ahead - first in a recess, then a line of flakes to finish up a rib.

There are two logical continuation scrambles. Across the shallow hollow of Cove Beck are the crags of Cove Rib, whilst if you walk further along the spur above Gill Cove Crags, the fine broad crags of

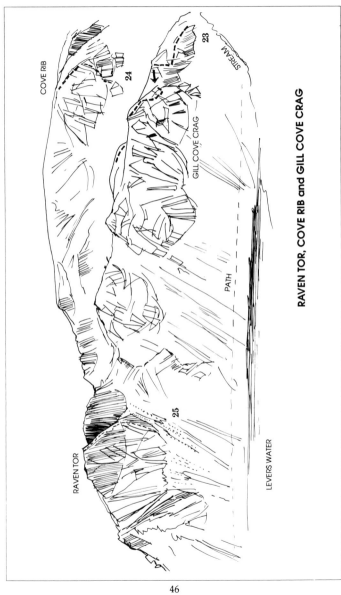

RAVEN TOR, COVE RIB and GILL COVE CRAG

COVE RIB

24

23

STREAM

GILL COVE CRAG

PATH

RAVEN TOR

25

LEVERS WATER

Raven Tor soon come into view.

24. COVE RIB   Grade 2*   SD 272992

A square crag, like a castle keep with many turrets, is the most obvious feature of a line of broken crags on the Brim Fell flank of Gill Cove.

Approach: From the previous scramble, or by the path towards Levers Hause until the upper combe of Gill Cove can be entered, where the rocks are seen on the right.

Character: The buttress appears too steep for scrambling, but the route unfolds on good rock well supplied with sharp holds and pockets, to finish up a fine crest. Slow drying due to its shady aspect, but the rock is more typical of the Coniston area than that of Gill Cove Crags below.

The Route: The scramble follows the left edge of the initial steep buttress, then continues along a series of sharp ribs. Ascend between two small lower crags to the left side of the main crag. There is a cairn

COVE RIB

24

at the foot of the rib. Climb easily for 25ft to a steepening. Step left onto a flake and mantelshelf over the bulge onto a rock shelf - or more easily gain the same ledge by a traverse from the left. Traverse right to a grass ledge and continue diagonally right to gain a rib. After a few feet move left of the steep prong and climb steeply on good holds about 20ft left of the arête. This concludes the first steep buttress.

The squat slabby rib straight ahead has a delicate mossy patch about 25ft up. An easier route lies up a gully on its right, but beware of the first chockstone which appears precariously balanced. The ridge ahead is gained by a traverse across a pocketed slab from the grass gully on the left. Climb a tower on its left side. Where the ridge fizzles out, cross left to reach a parallel spur which prolongs the scramble towards the ridge of Brim Fell.

The scramble on Raven Tor can be quickly reached by descending the spur from Brim Fell to the col at the top of the tor.

25. RAVEN TOR   Grade 3s*   SD 276989

Unless you are aware of them the crags of Raven Tor are easily overlooked. Although they form the northern flank of the spur above Levers Water, the crags are only fully seen from the far end of the lake. The rocks rise diagonally up the hillside, with the longest, cleanest, continuous rocks up to the right.

Approach: Steep screes at the side of the rocks above Levers Water lead directly to the scramble, or more easily, after either of the two preceding routes, the scramble can be approached by a descent from the col at the top of the crag.

Character: Although there is much scrappy rock on the buttresses, most of it is very solid and an army of jug handle flakes appears to be marching up the crags. There is scope for scrappy scrambling almost anywhere, but the route described is a logical one. There is little variety, but the good rock and exposed feel of a big crag makes it worthwhile. Although the holds are excellent, scrambling here is serious, for the whole crag is quite large - over 400ft high - and to be

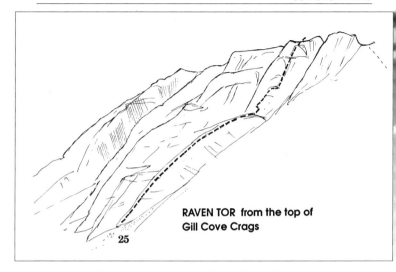

RAVEN TOR from the top of
Gill Cove Crags

25

safe it should be treated as a roped climb. The rocks steepen towards the top and care must be taken not to stray from the easiest route. The rest of the crag has much loose rock and should be avoided.

The Route: The broadest buttress in the centre of the crags lies left of a red scree shoot. In its upper part the right edge of the buttress is defined by a gully. This route takes the right edge of the central buttress, first overlooking the scree shoot, then the gully. The start is marked by a small cairn a little up the screes from the lowest rocks. The rib above the cairn gives very easy scrambling on solid flakes of rock overlooking the screes, for 160 feet to a steeper exit onto a diagonal rake.

From the topmost point of this, overlooking the gully, there is a fine sweep of steeper slabs. Climb these by the easiest zig-zag route - up for 20ft, then left to gain a groove which slants back right to a ledge. Move right along this then continue steeply up mossier rocks about 20ft left of the edge to a shelf about 140ft above the rake. Easier angled, clean rocks above lead directly to the top in a further 100ft.

26. LONG CRAG BUTTRESS   Grade 1**   SD 299981

Long Crag guards the entrance to the Coppermines Valley and overlooks Coniston village. The rocks are well broken, easy-angled and almost gabbro-like in texture - a good recipe for scrambling. The most continuous rock is a buttress at the left-hand side of the crags, which this route takes, whilst further right another sweep of rocks provide good entertainment. A feature of the rocks between is a striking columnar structure, almost like the basalt of Staffa.

Only a few minutes walk from Coniston, this scramble makes a fine start to a day in the Coniston fells.

Approach: Park in the village, either at the official car park (small fee) or alternatively there is plenty of parking by the old railway station. Immediately north of the bridge in the centre of the village, a lane runs by the river towards Coppermines Valley. Shortly after the tarmac ends, go through a gate and mount the open fell to the base of the spur. The best introductory rocks lie above and left of a tree.

Character: Superb rasp-rough rock, easy-angled and plenty of choice, with good positive holds.

The Route: The base of the first slabs contain a piton, and there is another at the top - a legacy of mountain rescue practice. Climb the slabs, walk up the spur for a 100 feet then move left to gain a string of mossy outcrops.

Climb the slabs right of a small holly tree, moving right near the top to clean slabs. A steep little prow above is best avoided on its left. Continue on the crest of light coloured slabs to the foot of the steeper upper buttress.

A rib curls into the steeper rocks, but holds are excellent and friction superb. At a grass ledge move right onto rough slabs which run diagonally leftwards up a ramp and the rib on its right.

Cross the grass gully on the right above a juniper, to climb the faceted slabs above. Where the angle eases the scrambling can be prolonged by traversing right to rocks overlooking the edge of the steep right-hand wall.

LONG CRAG

26   27

The top of the crags form the edge of a broad rocky plateau with the bulk of Wetherlam behind. To continue the day s scrambling it is best to head for a flat shelf on the left, above the entrance to the valley, where a path is picked up leading below the old quarries to contour the hillside into Red Dell. The leat below Kernel Crag can be followed to Levers Water and the wealth of scrambling around there, or Red Dell can be followed to Low Wether Crags at its head.

27. LONG CRAG - BOULDER ROUTE   Grade 2*   SD 299980
Despite some walking which splits the scramble into two sections, the rock is good and the scrambling very pleasant; just a touch more difficult than the previous route.

Approach: As for the previous route, but just where the tarmac ends go over a stile on the right and go diagonally across the hillside to the foot of the first slabs.

Character: Open slabby scrambling on superb rough rock.

The Route: About 50ft above an oak at the right-hand side of the slabs, is a rib by the side of a gully. Mount boulders at the start of the rib, then mossy slabs diagonally left a few feet until it is possible to climb more or less direct to a flat grass platform with several square-cut boulders.

The continuation of the scramble lies well above on a buttress left of a scree gully and right of a patch of junipers. A path leads right through the boulders and across the foot of the screes to mount a parallel grassy trough. Return left to the scree gully at its narrowest point - the rocks on its left are mossy and not worth bothering with. Ascend the gully for about 150ft then go left past a prominent yew to reach the more continuous clean slabs on the crest of the spur.

The slabs provide good scrambling in the centre, away from easy ground on the left. Where they fizzle out, move 20ft left to another slabby rib. Pass a terrace with gnarled junipers and mount a series of steep steps in the wall above (or pass on the left more easily). A steeper tower can be turned or climbed. Ahead climb slabs on the left of a juniper then bear right to reach the final rock buttress which gives a fine finish.

28. PUSSIE'S PARADISE, YEWDALE   Grade 2   NY 313003

A short scramble which is best done after Raven Crag, Yewdale (described in the original *Scrambles*).

Approach: From the top of the Raven Crag scramble, at about the same level to the right, at the head of a slight combe, is a small triangular crag of clean rock. A direct approach can be made by the climbers' path - over the stile near the highest point of the road below the crags. Walk right just above the wall where a very steep path ascends below the impending wall of Raven Crag. Cross right to the parallel combe and the crag.

Character: Short but interesting on good rock. Belays are scarce for roped ascents, but the main difficulty is near the start.

The Route: The foot of a clean columnar rib forms a small nook. Climb

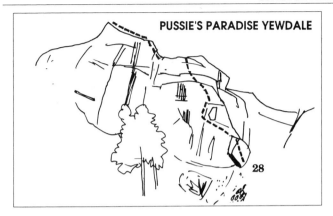

PUSSIE'S PARADISE YEWDALE

28

the front block 15ft, then make a long step left onto the steep wall. Move left to the base of a dangerous perched block. Avoid it by a step left onto a ledge. Continue above the block on a gangway leftwards to a grass shelf. Climb a ridge to another shelf. There is a heathery wall on the left and an easy outcrop to finish.

29. CHURCH BECK, CONISTON   Grade 1*   SD 297977
A surprisingly good trip with a striking ravine, several waterfalls and deep pools.

Approach: Park up the Walna Scar road or by the old railway station. Go up a lane left of the Sun Hotel and the path which follows, signed YH.' Go through a meadow and where the rough lane rises steeply gain Church Beck at a bridge on the right.

Character: Church Beck usually carries a lot of water. This trip is only feasible in a long dry spell. The rocks are smooth and slippery. Be prepared for some shallow wading. Some of the pools are popular bathing spots for village children.

The Route: The first cascade is soon reached, the rock bed fretted and scoured into attractive shapes. Reach a weir in a sylvan setting. Gain the central rib and go left up the dry river bed. The walls converge into a gorge, entered by a shallow wade on the left-hand side. Pass under a fallen tree in this impressive defile and climb slabs by the side of a cascade. Cross to the right to bypass a pool. Another waterfall is climbed on its left to reach yet another fall, unfortunately impassable between steep walls with a deep pool at its base. Return to the lip of the previous fall and escape right (facing downstream). A slight path in the bracken joins the lane above. Regain the stream by a ledge just below Miners' Bridge. On the left is an old mine level which can be explored if you have a torch. It begins with a wade. See *Coniston Copper Mines - A Field Guide by* Eric Holland (Cicerone Press).

The rocks of the fall can be bypassed, or climbed at a much higher grade than the rest of the trip. Wade to the central rib, climb up to the right side of a prow and ascend the vertical right wall of this on widely spaced holds, good at the top (Gr.3).

Pass under the bridge to another small ravine. Where it twists to reveal a cascade, exit on a ramp on the right. Regain the bed and round the corner is a final cascade, easily climbed.

The flat floor of the Coppermines Valley lies ahead.

RED DELL

Whilst the scrambling possibilities of the ravine and waterslide slabs above the mine building look enticing, the ravine has an impassable fall and the waterslide slabs are coated with a broad veneer of slippery gunge. It is better to walk up the path!

30. MOULDRY BANK and RASCAL HOW   Grade 2   SD 295981

An easily accessible scramble which can make a good start to a day in the Coniston Fells, although not as good as the neighbouring route on Long Crags.

Approach: Park in Coniston village by the old railway station at the start of the Walna Scar road. Follow the track towards the Coppermines Valley, signed to the 'YH,' to Miners' Bridge, where it joins the other rough road on the other side of the stream. Mouldry Bank is the rocky spur above the road on the east side of the stream. From the

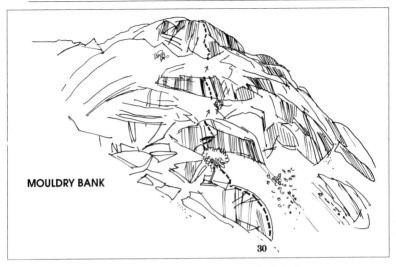

MOULDRY BANK

30

bridge slant diagonally right to the lowest rock rib below a tree.

Character: A logical line up a series of rock steps on quite good rock.

The Route: Climb the rib and pass the tree on the right. Gain a vegetated recess in the steep barrier ahead and move right to cross a bulge on good holds (avoidable left). An easy-angled rock tongue points the way past a tree to a steeper wall. Walk to the foot of the cleanest section of the final rocks and start at the lowest point. Climb 15ft to a groove which slants left. Holds are excellent. The angle now eases to the top of the knoll, where the next rocks can be seen across a dip.

Head for the toe of an obvious buttress. The scrambling is on a thin rib with one or two tricky moves. Near the top traverse right below vegetation into an earthy gully and easy ground.

Return to the dip between the two sections of the scramble, where a path right soon joins a quarry track which descends to the main path up the eastern side of the Coppermines Valley above Irish Row.

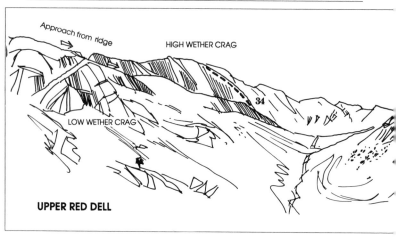

At the top of Red Dell waterslide note the abundant evidence of old mining activity. Above and right of the old masonry tower is the Old Engine Shaft of Bonsor Mine. If you have a torch it is worth going just into the tunnel to the edge overlooking the balance bob platform. Across this is the 1,395ft deep shaft! For further information about the mines in the Coniston area see *Coniston Copper Mines - A Field Guide* by Eric Holland (Cicerone Press).

Kennel Crag lies ahead on the end of the ridge. It has an impressive pinnacle but is not suitable for scrambling. If you are heading for Upper Red Dell continue directly up the valley bottom; if you are going towards Levers Water cross the col directly below Kennel Crag to join a horizontal track which joins the pony track to Levers Water. Going this way, the scrambler can continue along a little used pony track towards Levers Water Beck and incorporate the best bit of that route.

31. SUNLIGHT SLABS   Grade 2   SD 282994

On the right-hand (east) side of Levers Water is a tumble of ribs and slabs. This scrambles takes more or less the prominent rib, although other ways can be found.

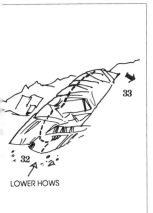

Character: Good rock but the best route involves using small holds and rock climbing situations. Short but pleasant. Disjointed if easier ways are sought.

The Route: Start at the foot of a prominent long rib. Avoid the first steep section by the gully on its right then ascend the arête with an excursion onto the easier ground on the right. From a terrace the rib is climbed on its left side.

This leads to the ridge above Red Dell. The scramble on High Wether Crag can be reached by ascending the ridge for about half a mile to a flat platform high on the ridge just below a rocky step. The terrace right leads below the crags to the scramble.

UPPER RED DELL
The upper part of Red Dell is one of the least visited corners of the Coniston Fells, the path up the valley is slight, the valley head a wall of crag, especially on the left. The first vegetated crag, Erin Crag, is not fit for scrambling. Low Wether Crag is too fierce but the more amenable angle of High Wether Crags invites attention. Well above the sheepfold, on the hillside right of the stream is the compact knot of Lower Hows.

32. LOWER HOWS   Grade 2*   NY 286003
Character: The best type of Coniston rock - slabs the texture of gabbro, so rough that the experienced scrambler can enjoy this route in rain. A good way to the top of the Lad Stones Ridge of Wetherlam.

The Route: Start at the lowest point of a broad slabby base, cairn. Go direct for 60ft then left below the overhang to easier ground. Continue to a shelf. Ascend rocks about 10ft left of a fine arête and follow the easiest route to a terrace. A crack splits an overhang. Climb to the base of the crack then avoid it by the slab on the right. The angle eases but slabs give good scrambling well up the hillside.

33. UPPER HOWS   Grade 2   NY 287004

Descending slightly from the top of the main rocks of the previous scramble, across the hillside to the right is another crag, which is steep in its lower part. There is a messy gully just left of the lowest rocks which can be used to gain 20ft or so, after which traverse rightwards to gain clean, easy ground. The rocks are followed pleasantly until they peter out not far from the Wetherlam ridge footpath.

To the right of Lower Hows, (NY 288001) several hundred yards down the valley is another three tier succession of craglets which give a mild scramble.

LOW WETHER CRAG high on the left looks promising but is too difficult for scrambling. There is a Difficult' climb up the most prominent buttress on the right, cairn at base, rarely visited.

34. HIGH WETHER CRAG   Grade 2   NY 284006

This lies above a grass terrace high on the left side of the valley. The rock here is better and a scramble feasible at its right end.

Approach: Either by a very steep ascent from the valley floor or more easily from the ridge where a flat terrace below a rock barrier leads right below the crags. Start at the right-hand end.

Character: An open, exposed scramble on good rock which eases after a steep start.

The Route: Start below a rock rib with a small pedestal at its foot, just left of the right-hand end of the crags. Cairn. Climb the prow for 30ft to a bilberry ledge. Go diagonally left then back right across a grass ledge to easier angled rocks. Good scrambling straight ahead, passing two grass ledges. After about 100ft move right for 30ft, below a steepening, to a rib which fizzles out in grassy slopes.

The summit of Wetherlam is a short walk away.

35. CONISTON OLD MAN, SOUTH SIDE - GOAT CRAG
Grade 1*   SD 268974

An easy scramble up a fellside littered with small craglets provides an unusual route up the Old Man.

Approach: Park just inside the fell gate at the start of the rough road to Walna Scar. Before Torver Beck take the path right towards Goat's Water. Where the path levels the craggy hillside can be seen ahead just above the path. Pass mine spoils and 400 metres past a white cairn the path turns left below the jumble of rocks. Start just past a small stream where boulders reach the path.

Character: Knobbly rock gives a firm footing even when damp. Flake handholds are found in abundance but their tops are thin and friable - take care. The route is not at all serious but height is gained with interest. The craglets follow in rapid succession with little walking

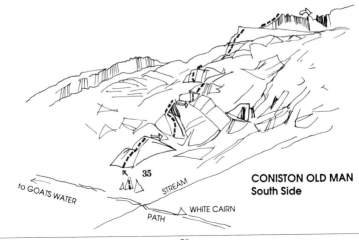

CONISTON OLD MAN
South Side

between, and can be varied at will.

The Route: Start at the second of two small outcrops - a short pocketed slab. Walk left to larger slabs, (cairn below left end). Climb either side of a recess, the right side is more difficult. Straight up easy-angled slab above. Climb a steep flaky wall at the right end of the next outcrop. A rib leads into a deep groove in the block above. Ascend a slabby rib on the left then go diagonally left to below a steep face. Go left along a rock ledge to easy spiky rocks. Just above, an outcrop is climbed by a smooth groove to emerge on the right. Climb the spiky ridge ahead onto the pyramid-shaped rock so noticeable from the base.

Where the ridge levels out to merge into the fellside go left below crags. Climb the edge by a shattered rib. Broken rocks continue for a considerable way up the fellside - go leftwards for the best route - a short chimney with earthy footholds, a corner crack, a face and a crack with a difficult start. Above this the rocks fizzle out onto the summit slopes of the Old Man.

36. EASTER GULLY and INTERMEDIATE GULLY, DOW CRAG
Grade 3*   SD 264976
This is a climber's scramble up the middle of Dow Crag, in impressive rock surroundings.

Approach: Follow the approach described above but continue along the path to Goat's Water, where a track up the scree leads to the base of the crags. Easter Gully is the deepest V-shaped gully in the centre of the crags, just right of the narrow squat D-Buttress and left of the broad broken E-Buttress.

Character: Some people claim this is one of their favourite scrambles, but in all but perfect conditions it is unbelievably green and greasy. It is a climbers' descent route. Not one of my choice! The crux of Easter Gully is strenuous and forbidding. A climbers' route. Serious.

The Route: Scramble into the base of the greasy gully and struggle past a small chock into a bay below a huge impressive wedged block. This forms the crux of the route and needs a bold layback move around the left side of the block. Above is another amphitheatre below a steep pear-shaped crag which has several classic rock climbs.

Scramble up left onto the end of Easy Terrace (which constitutes the alternative climbers' descent route left). Go along this to the first major gully above. This is the upper part of Intermediate Gully - the lower half is a severe and strenuous climb. Ascend the gully, which has a couple of small pitches, to the top.

37. LONG CRAG, WETHERLAM   Grade 1/2*   NY 284017
This lies on the Greenburn face of Wetherlam, a long route in a secluded situation.

Approach: From Fell Foot Bridge in Little Langdale. The best parking places lie further up the road past the farm. Take the track past Bridge End to join the old mine track up the valley. At the mines the driest route takes the right fork, to keep close to the stream. Cross the embankment of the usually dry lake. The scramble starts straight ahead up a craggy spur.

Character: A succession of craglets mount a long spur. Where this merges into the hillside the route takes the right side of the broken crag to the left. A long scramble, about 1,000ft vertical height, disjointed in parts and open to much variation. The rock is rough and solid, clean where it catches the afternoon sun, but green and slow drying in the shade. An interesting, unusual way up Wetherlam, with fine views.

The Route: Start at the foot of the spur directly above the tarn, at a nose of rock between two trees. Cairn. Climb the steep nose and easy-angled slabs. Go slightly right to a smooth green scoop. Move left below a steep block to climb the left edge of a short chockstone chimney, then through boulders and up slabs and a crest to the top of the first knoll.

Ahead is the next craglet, too steep at its left end, but with a right

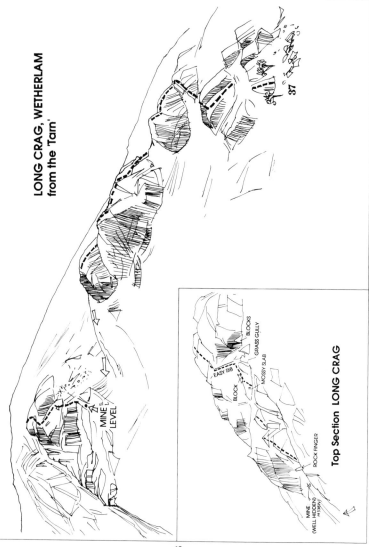

LONG CRAG, WETHERLAM
from the Tarn'

37

MINE LEVEL

Top Section LONG CRAG

BLOCKS

GRASS GULLY

EASY RIB

MOSSY SLAB

BLOCK

ROCK FINGER

MINE
(WELL HIDDEN)
(+30m)

slanting ridge below. Follow the ridge and near its top climb the clean nose on the left.

The next craglet lies across a gully and has some interesting rock. There is a prominent knife edge rib which is gained by crossing the grass gully. Reach the edge from a ledge on its right and climb the ridge. Move left across a gully onto clean slabs to the top of a pointed rock. (Another way gains this point more directly by a shallow groove.) Stride boldly across the gap.

Go straight ahead up grass and boulders then up a groove, steep to start, in a slabby outcrop. Move horizontally left to easy-angled slabs of perfect rock with many options, to the top of the long spur.

Ahead rise scree slopes to the summit plateau, but on the left is a jumble of steep crag which hosts the final section of the scramble. Take care to locate the correct route - if you stray too far left the rock is more vegetated and greasy.

Walk left across two scree spoil heaps. Just past these another small scree comes from a gully. Look up to locate a small drystone wall, with a mine trial level hidden above. The scramble restarts on the rock rib to its left.

Climb the rib, first left then right, then straight ahead. On the left is a bilberry groove, climb this by its left slabby side. Up grass to a moss-speckled slab. Climb the centre of this to a ledge with a large boulder. Escape right onto a long easy rib to a grass ledge up left. Go back right up a short slanting crack and follow further slabby rocks to the top.

Wetherlam summit lies a short walk above.

Other scrambles on the Greenburn face of Great Carrs (described in the original *Scrambles*) are easily reached from Swirl Hause.

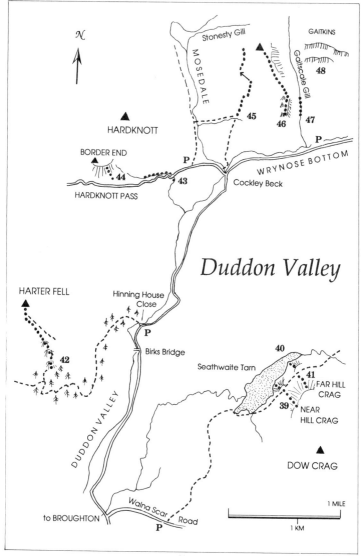

Esk Gorge, Eskdale. Bill Todd on two of the numerous incidents of this excellent trip.

Duddon Valley

The gentle beauty of the Duddon Valley is typical of Lakeland scenery at its best - an inspiring blend of colourful woodland, rock outcrops and rough fell, with a backdrop of higher fells to round off the scene. There are no major crags, no major villages and only a narrow tortuous road traverses the valley floor. It remains the least spoilt of the Lakeland valleys and offers a peaceful sanctuary from the more popular centres.

Some of the best scrambling is centred on the little side valley of Seathwaite and the craggy end of Crinkle Crags which overlooks the head of the Duddon. The rock is generally firm, rough and clean; a good recipe for an enjoyable outing.

There is a campsite at Turner Hall Farm, near Seathwaite.

38. WHITE PIKE   Grade 1   SD 247953

Few people know this summit for it is merely the end of the ridge south of the Walna Scar track, yet from the southern fringes of the Lakes its steep profile is quite distinctive.

Approach: About half a mile past Seathwaite fork right, signed Coniston. Unfit for cars.' Keep straight on at a junction and park through a gate at the start of the Walna Scar track. Follow the track until below the first quarry spoil heap where a green track slants right to a gate. Turn right on a horizontal track above the wall, past old quarry buildings. Fork left on a faint green track just past the spoil heaps and follow this round the hillside through a little gap with a fine view seawards. The path continues around the hillside and the crags soon come into view. The scramble takes what appears to be a long broken skyline ridge.

Character: Disjointed, but good in parts on generally good rock, although care is required in places. Slippery when damp.

A traverse above a deep pool on the Esk Gorge

The Route: When below the crags look for a prominent knob with an overhang below its top left edge. Below and left of this the best starting rocks are on a narrow rib which rises from a patch of bracken. Mount the edge of scree to its base.

Climb shattered rock up the front to a grass ledge at 20ft. Move left for 15ft onto slabs and ascend these to a grass terrace. You could continue directly, but a longer and more interesting diversion is to incorporate the prominent knob which lies to the right. Descend to the very foot of this and climb a steep edge, moving left onto the rock edge where the angle eases. At the top go left across grass to another rock spur.

Move onto the front by a small shelf then keep more or less to the crest of the spur, with odd steepenings and some walking before a definite steeper knoll is reached. Ascend by a groove in the middle and more shattered rocks to the top.

The summit (1,960ft) is a fine viewpoint and almost certainly you will have the place to yourself. Descent can be made along the ridge towards Walna Scar or drop left to the quarry, avoiding the old workings, which are dramatic in places.

The ridge to the south of White Peak is quite shapely, with the pyramid of **Caw** (1,735ft) and the sharp **Stickle Pike** (1,231ft) prominent. There is a wealth of rock, and a surplus of bracken, although little tracks criss-cross the area. Some scrambling of a disjointed nature could be worked out, especially from the valley road just south of Ulpha, where the rocky slopes of Yew Barrow could make an interesting approach to Stickle Pike.

SEATHWAITE TARN

The most concentrated collection of scrambles in the Duddon is found in the secluded side valley which holds Seathwaite Tarn. Some good routes are described in the previous volume of *Scrambles* on the crags around Tarn Beck and Little Blake Rigg. The routes described here make excellent continuations at a similar standard.

The setting is peaceful and emphasises that it is easy to find both beauty and solitude on the busiest of summer weekends. The following routes lie on the south-east side of Seathwaite Tarn where crags tumble to the lake shore. A small path traverses well above the lake.

39. SHUDDERSTONE HOW and NEAR HILL CRAG
Grade 2**   NY 255987
From the dam Shudderstone How is the prominent knoll which rises out of the water about half-way along the lake.

Approach: About half a mile past Seathwaite a small lane forks right, signed Walna Scar. Follow this, right at a fork, for ¹/2 mile to park just through the fell gate. Take the waterworks road, left through a gate, and follow it rising gently to the dam at the outlet to Seathwaite Tarn. A slight path goes around the right side of the lake to cross the col at the head of Shudderstone How. Leave the path before this and drop to lake level, to pass below one rib to another out of sight of the path. Start at a rock outcrop at water level. Cairn.

Character: Excellent rough rock, but it becomes very slippery when wet. The route links the most attractive pitches and although devious at times, is quite interesting.

The Route: Go leftwards up the slab to a steep exit. Continue up easier rocks overlooking the edge on the right. At its top descend grass to the base of the main sweep of slabs just to the right. The front of this makes a fine pitch, cairn. Climb a grass groove for 10ft then up the rib on the right. Step onto a grass ledge right and regain the rib which gives excellent scrambling to a mossy slab. At a flat grass platform go up a clean prow in the centre of the bay to the top of the How.

In the gap is a large square boulder. Mount the slab behind this and walk left to the right end of a steep wall above boulders. Climb the right-hand block by thin twin cracks. Keep left on the edge of the rock to a grass platform.

Ascend the next slabs up the middle to below a steep slabby wall which is beyond the scope of scrambling. An unsatisfactory messy route can be made left of the steep rocks but a far more interesting, though devious, route is as follows.

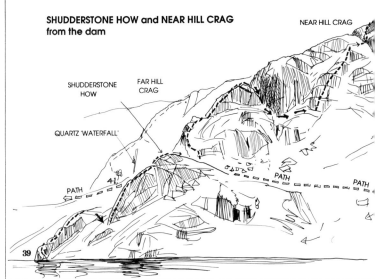

SHUDDERSTONE HOW and NEAR HILL CRAG
from the dam

NEAR HILL CRAG

SHUDDERSTONE
HOW

FAR HILL
CRAG

QUARTZ 'WATERFALL'

PATH

PATH

PATH

41

39

Descend the short gully on the right to the base of the steep rocks.
(This point can be reached with less interest from half-way up the
slabs along a terrace.) Walk well to the right below the steep crag past
a mossy section to more amenable rocks, cairn. Climb a clean rib to
a steeper wall and escape right to rocks on the side of a grassy gully
and back left. On the right a sweep of quartz-flecked slabs lead on.
Where they peter out move left onto more slabs and walls. Near the
top move left along a grass ledge to a good steep rib.

Above is a prominent steep prow with a bulging block at its foot. This
section is exposed and some people may feel the need of a safety rope.
From the base of the block move right along an airy ledge and up to
a grass platform. Move back left onto the arête with some suspect
rock in an exposed position. Follow the edge to the top.

Goat's Hause lies an almost horizontal walk across the fell to the left.

40. RAVEN NEST HOW   Grade 2**   SD 258992
The next steep knoll near the head of the tarn, looks formidable but
yields a little gem.

Approach: As the previous route, but continue along the path and drop to the lake level.

Character: Steep and exposed but perfect rough rock with good holds.

The Route: Start at the right-hand corner of the crag at a slab about 15ft left of the edge. The first 15 feet is quite tricky but soon eases. Move right to the edge and gain a grass ledge. Step steeply back left onto slabs and left a few feet into a steep corner. Climb this up the side of a detached block. An exposed ledge leads horizontally left to the front. Finish by rocks on the left of the arête.

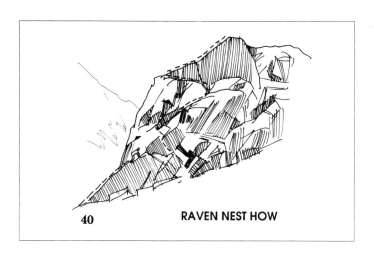

40   **RAVEN NEST HOW**

41. FAR HILL CRAG   Grade 2**   SD 258988

This lies above Raven Nest How and forms the logical continuation, again on good rough rock. On the right side of the crags is a

The final knobby pitch on Far Hill Crag

prominent quartz band which from a distance looks like a thin cascade. This ribbon is unattractive for scrambling, but an excellent route starts a little below it.

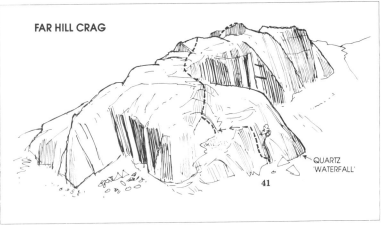

FAR HILL CRAG

QUARTZ 'WATERFALL'

41

The Route: Start in a steep groove about 20ft below a rowan, and step onto slabs on the left. Continue past the tree to the top of the first rib. On the left is a grass patch below the steep side wall of an arête. Go to the top corner of this patch to ascend a steep cracked wall for 15ft onto the arête. Follow a series of short steep walls to a grass terrace below a steep crag. Climb a subsidiary rib to gain slabs at a mossy recess, just left of the steeper crag. Above is a slab of strange whorls which provide small but good holds.

42. HARTER FELL (2,140ft) by BRANDY CRAGS
 Grade 2** SD 223988

The south-east slopes of Duddon's Harter Fell are peppered with rock outcrops of excellent quality. Many scrambles can be devised but the one described here is probably the most continuous. Brandy Crag is a steep square-cut castle-shaped outcrop just above the forest and a succession of smaller craglets lead on to the summit. The walking between is never more than a few minutes.

Approach: From the pleasantly situated riverside car park at Hinning House Close, 200 yards north of Birks Bridge, take the road over the river and rise gently past Birks. Take an uphill right fork and where the road doubles back the crag pokes into view above the trees. At the next bend leave the road and mount a grassy break, bear right to the foot of the first steep crags.

Character: Brandy Crag is a steep knoll which can be ascended at various grades of difficulty. There are several obvious rock climbing pitches up its challenging front - a gangway slanting left to right, a steep groove on its right, and a direct route from the middle of the gangway. The route described is a grade 2 scramble. On the succeeding outcrops many variations are possible to suit your taste. Good solid rock throughout, although it is unpleasantly slippery when wet.

The Route: An obvious feature of the crag is a gangway slanting left to right. Right is a deep groove with easier angled slabs to its right.

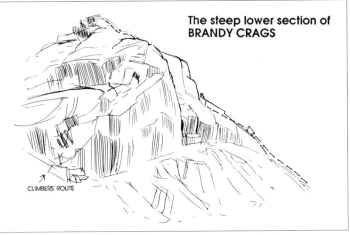

The steep lower section of BRANDY CRAGS

CLIMBERS' ROUTE

The route takes these slabs and avoids the steeper rock above.

Start below the frontal slabs and scramble up easy rocks to a perched block at the foot of the clean sweep of slabs. Go delicately diagonally left along a break for 40ft towards the deep groove. (Do not go too far, for the groove bristles with overlaps.) Easy slabs allow a rising traverse back right and across a little gangway below a steepening to gain a grassy groove round the corner. Step back left onto the slabs and climb to a grass neck above the steep initial crags. Another belt of rough slabs completes this first section, the only serious part of the trip.

The next rocks lie two minutes' walk ahead. Aim for the lowest bouldery rocks on the left. Climb two large boulders to their exposed top whence a cracked slab makes a delicate finish. Immediately right is a grey block. Climb this left to right, to face a long low wall of crag ahead. Walk right 100ft to below a twin buttress split by a bilberry gully. Mount the broad shelf to the right of the gully and continue up broken ribs.

The next small outcrop has a tiny pointed block at its foot. Climb directly from this then walk right to the foot of a steep skyline turret. A groove at the lowest point of this is climbed awkwardly.

Ahead another low outcrop is best climbed at its left. Across an intervening dip lie the summit rocks. Join a path left towards the skyline outcrops. Start scrambling again at a rock tooth just by the path. After another slabby knoll, cross the slabs to the foot of the final rock tor, to the right of the trig. point which lies on a lower more accessible top. The most satisfying finish is by a crack which splits the steep wall. This is much easier than it looks. Other alternatives abound.

43. HARDKNOTT GILL   Grade 1   NY 238016

A pretty little gill which provides a modest easy scramble. It can be combined with the scramble up Border End.

Start where the Hardknott Pass road crosses the gill on the Duddon Valley side. There is a good parking place below the bridge.

Scramble up to the bridge, go through the culvert and continue up the narrow ravine. There are short stretches or rock scrambling interspersed with boulder hopping and walking. The ravine opens out and at a sharp right bend, go out of the gill left to reach the road.

44. BORDER END   Grade 1   NY 231016

An easy scramble on good rough rock, ideal as a continuation to the preceding route.

The summit of the Hardknott road pass is crowned by a large cairn, just below which on the Esk side is a small parking place. The scramble starts opposite this.

Surmount a steep little wall, then walk left towards a prominent rock spur with a steep right wall. Scramble up the front of this spur on lovely rough rock, by a succession of shelves and steps to the summit plateau.

It is worth going to the far cairn overlooking Eskdale for the spectacular view across the valley to the Scafell peaks.

45. LITTLE STAND   Grade 2**   NY 248026

The steep, rocky southern arm of Crinkle Crags drops into the head of the Duddon Valley overlooking Cockley Beck. The scope for

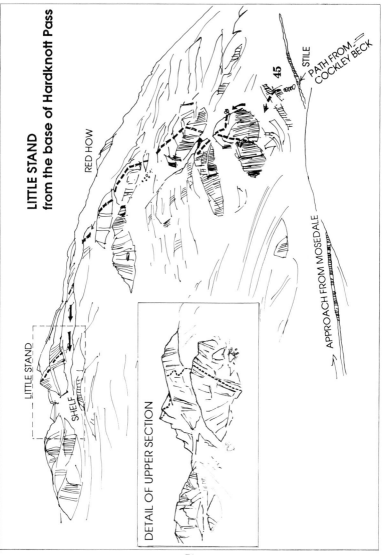

LITTLE STAND
from the base of Hardknott Pass

RED HOW

45

STILE

PATH FROM
COCKLEY BECK

APPROACH FROM MOSEDALE

LITTLE STAND

SHELF

DETAIL OF UPPER SECTION

scrambling is broad - another route is described on Red How on the eastern side of the mountain - but the following route takes a logical line with a minimum of walking between rocks and has a fine finish up the sharp rocks of Little Stand (2,427ft). The walk along the almost flat summit ridge is very attractive, with rock outcrops mirrored in reedy pools; a fine way onto the Crinkles. A slight path follows the line of the scramble, but wends around the crags instead of up them.

Approach: Either park near Cockley Beck farm, cross the bridge, go over a stile on the right, across a tiny footbridge then strike up the fellside on a slight path to below the rocks - or, better, park a short way up the Hardknott road, where there is ample space, at the start of a path which traverses into Mosedale. Follow this path up the valley until level with the intake wall on the right. Cross the stream and keep above a fence to the foot of a prominent clean knott of rock on the skyline. It is just above a stile, where the direct path joins.

Character: A long scramble on sound, rough rock with a wide choice. The route seeks out a succession of rock knolls. Described as grade 2, but sections are easily bypassed and there is scope for more difficult climbing variations.

The Route: Start at a rib directly above the remains of a low stone wall. This soon steepens into difficulties, which are best avoided on the right to climb the wall just right of a spike. The steep crag lies above. On the left of the main face is a heathery break. Slant up this from left to right, past a steep block and left across a wall to a length of easier angled rough slabs to the top of the knoll. (An easier alternative gains the slabs by a ledge above a small ash half-way up the right side of the crag.)

Continue up the next knoll, then cross a gully to rocks on its right. Climb the left side of a steep rib (or the slabs to its right) to the next knoll. A broad crag bars the way ahead. A scrambling route lies on the right past a grass ledge to reach an easy-angled rib which develops into slabs to the next top.

Walk to a small craglet which leads to a broad grass shelf, where the summit crags of Little Stand are well displayed. To follow the

Near the top of Little Stand. Photo: A Evans

described route walk left along the shelf where the pyramid-shape of the final rock is seen (see sketch).

Start this section above the grass shelf at the larger, slightly higher of two outcrops, at a central rib (cairn). This crag is more continuous and exposed than anything preceding. The rib leads into slabs slanting right, past a line of perched blocks, to a flat rocky platform which hosts a small pool in wet weather. Scramble above the right end of the terrace, a series of steep walls with good holds, first by a rib into a groove, exit left round a block. The steep wall above is awkward.

Walk left to the foot of a pyramid of slabs and climb the front of these by a gangway. Finish easily round the rib left, or take a more difficult line up the steep front. Another pyramid ahead completes the route.

STONESTY GILL cuts into the steep flank of Stonesty Pike and Little Stand, on the eastern side of Mosedale. The gill appears to be a scrambling possibility but entices only to disappoint. The rock bed is very narrow and unless it is a very dry spell, will have too much water. The cascades prove too difficult to ascend direct and the rock is suspect in places. Not really worth investigating.

SWINSTY GILL just to the north, on the same hillside, cuts through a fine steep -walled ravine, but contains an unclimbable waterfall.

46. RED HOW from WRYNOSE BOTTOMS
 Grade 1* NY 255026
Red How is the craggy southern end of the Crinkle Crags ridge, overlooking Wrynose Bottoms at the head of the Duddon Valley. There is a lot of rock on a broad frontage, the route described takes a logical line up the right edge.

Approach: Park by the roadside in Wrynose Bottoms, opposite Gaitscale Gill, a popular picnic spot. There is a path by the side of the gill, then cross a stile left and go diagonally left over screes to the foot of the

RED HOW from Wrynose Bottoms

GAITSCALE GILL 47

46

rocks. Start well below a prominent slab at the lowest outcrop.

Character: A long scramble with some interesting sections but much of the route lies at a very easy angle. Good rock.

The Route: The first low wall is possible anywhere. A good start is by the left edge of a large flake.

The prominent slab with its grooved wall lies above. Mount slabs which run left to right below the steeper left wall. Reach the foot of these by a left leading ledge. Climb the rough slab diagonally right, then straight up the centre of the buttress.

At a flattish grass terrace go right to rocks overlooking the steep right wall. A mixture of rock walking and easy scrambling up ledgy slabs leads to a terrace below a more compact knot. Start at the lowest toe and climb clean rocks. A blunt rib gives delightful scrambling. After 40ft move right onto more clean rocks.

Ahead left of a grassy gully is another slab outcrop. Start up light slabs then move left onto the main slabs.

Walk on towards a steeper outcrop to the right of a grassy gully. Climb broken light coloured rocks to the base of a steep wall which is more difficult than anything else on the route (grade 2). Easier alternatives exist on the left of the grassy gully. The route gains a groove in the centre of the vertical wall by a traverse from the left across an overlap. Steep to start but good holds, an excellent pitch.

The route now reverts to easy scrambling/rock walking up the right edge of the grass gully towards a prominent skyline tooth. Move left at the head of the gully to a terrace below a steep rock wall. Climb this by a series of steps trending right. The fine slabs left of the tooth are climbed by the left side of a large flake.

The summit cairn lies close and the flat-topped ridge gives a pleasant walk onto Crinkle Crags.

47. GAITSCALE GILL   Grade 1   NY 256025

This stream makes a pleasant ascent to the crags of Gaitkins, although the scrambling is quite short. The gill runs down the eastern side of Red How, see above for approach.

The first ravine contains a waterslide but there is an impassable fall at its head. Another small ravine lies ahead.

48. GAITKINS

This is an area of many small crags in several tiers with scope for a pleasant afternoon's scrambling or climbing. The lowest tier has a steep buttress at its left end and easier rocks right. Above is a prominent red triangular slab, below and right of the summit. This leads to a broad band of red slabs below the summit, with a great choice of route.

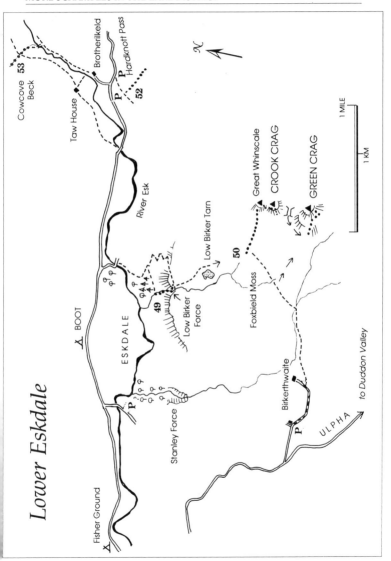

Lower Eskdale

A long quiet valley of great charm, Eskdale can be split into two distinct parts - the lower gentle valley, a colourful mix of trees, bracken and heather entwining numerous rock outcrops on low fells; and the upper valley - a rugged bare haven amongst the highest peaks of the area.

The scrambling in Eskdale is especially varied with a fine mixture of crags and gills, some in Lower Eskdale composed of granite, often smoother with less holds than the more conventional Lakeland volcanic rock, yet offering good sport. Otherwise the rock is as good as anywhere in the Lake District - rough, sound and with plenty of holds.

Lower Eskdale has a fine combination in Birker Force, followed by the scrambles on Crook Crag and Green Crag, as rocky as any summits in the Lakes. The Esk Gorge is a classic way to reach Upper Eskdale in a dry spell, whilst Cowcove Beck has its moments. There is something of excellence to suit all tastes in Eskdale.

There are campsites at Fisherground (near Eskdale Green) and Boot.

49. LOW BIRKER FORCE   Grade 3***   NY 186002
An excellent scramble which gives intimate views of one of Lakeland's most beautiful cascades. Low Birker Force lies on the steep southern slopes of Eskdale almost opposite Boot.

Approach: Just before the Woolpack Inn a lane branches right to Penny Hill. There is room to squeeze a car or two on the verge by the lane entrance and again a short way down the lane. Cross the fine old Doctor Bridge and go right on a rough lane to Low Birker. Just past the buildings fork sharp left on a lesser lane which zig-zags to a gate above a plantation. Go right along the wallside above the trees to enter the gill.

Starting the serious scrambling on Low Birker Force

Character: The first half of the scramble lies up a broad boulder floored stream bed in a deep-cut ravine, its sides a profusion of hollyhocks. The imposing headwall, down which the force leaps and bounds, appears impossible but is climbed on its left side to escape on a hidden ramp below the final steep barrier. The rock is granite, solid in the main, but care required in places. The main pitch is very exposed and a rope is advised. Whilst the scramble is possible in medium water levels, the rock is slippery where wet. Avoid if at all greasy- the rock takes a long time to dry.

The Route: A short defile is followed by a chaotic jumble of boulders large and small, which constitute the river bed. At a steep cascade climb a clean 30ft rib on the left, and round the corner the formidable headwall comes into view.

Scramble easily to the foot of the main falls and the start of the serious scrambling. Climb a slabby ramp on the left by a steep awkward corner to an easing of angle. Go up a steep rib to a small tree and move right to a ledge. Move up steeply again then climb the left wall to a small tree. Traverse right to a ledge below the final cascade. A direct ascent of the steep slimy rocks seems improbable but an escape is offered by a grassy ramp left.

Join a path along the top of the scarp. For a return go left along this to reach an old zig-zag pony track (the old peat road) which descends to Low Birker.

Continuation scrambles on Crook Crag and Green Crag are reached by going right along the path above the force to follow the stream past Low Birker Tarn. The foot of the Great Whinscale ridge lies across the boggy hollow.

CROOK CRAG and GREEN CRAG (1,602ft)

These two peaks, along with many subsidiary knobbles, form a striking rock ridge which rises from the boggy moorland of Ulpha. Although of very modest height, they provide a surprising wealth of good scrambling on excellent rough rock. The Great Whinscale route on Crook Crag gives a scramble of 600 feet vertical height. Combined with a scramble on Green Crag, another 400 feet vertical height, this

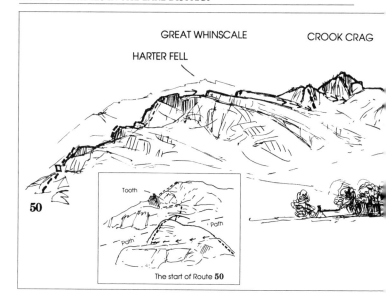

The start of Route **50**

gives a very satisfying outing, useful when higher peaks are in cloud.

Character: The scrambling is very open, exposed in places - which accounts for the grade of 2 - generally with plenty of choice. The described routes take the most logical lines on interesting rock. The holds are positive and solid, with only a few loose blocks, whilst friction is generally good. However the coating of lichen renders the rock slippery soon after rain.

The scrambles culminate on the summits, which must be counted amongst the nicest rock peaks in the Lakes.

50. CROOK CRAG by GREAT WHINSCALE
Grade 2** SD 194991

Seen from the Ulpha road, Crook Crag is the left-hand, northerly peak of the two. The route more or less follows the skyline ridge, then ascends The Pike by its right-hand ridge.

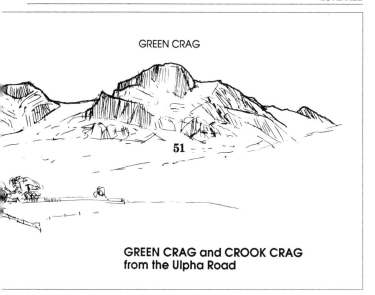

GREEN CRAG

51

**GREEN CRAG and CROOK CRAG
from the Ulpha Road**

Approach: Car based scramblers can approach from the Ulpha road. Take the minor branch lane towards Stanley Force but park on the grass verge at the start of the private road on the right to Birkerthwaite. Walk almost to Birkerthwaite and where the lane turns towards the farm, continue straight ahead on the right of a wire fence and over a stile. Another stile ahead gives access to a boggy moss. Cross Smallstone Beck and continue along the flat moss, driest on its right edge. Fox Bield, a little rock island amongst the bog myrtle, is passed and the start of the scramble can be identified. A landmark is a small tooth-like protuberance on the lower skyline ridge. The route starts on rocks below and right of this. From the moss mount a heathery rise and cross to the foot of the lowest rocks.

The same point can be reached from Eskdale by either of the two old peat roads. The one from Low Birker, which mounts steeply onto the boggy shelf by Low Birker Tarn leads to the foot of the rocks. The best approach of all is by the scramble up Low Birker Force (Gr.3).

The Route: The lowest rocks, right of the prominent skyline tooth, form a little knoll. Start up the right edge to a grass shelf. Walk left to rocks on the left edge. The next rocks are climbed on the right, by slabs to the left of a smooth slab. Mount a pile of blocks to a grass terrace and walk left to the tooth. This is climbed direct, or a step left half-way onto a little gangway gives more interest. Now take rocks on the right to a terrace.

The rock pillar ahead is easier than it appears and is climbed straight up the front on good holds. Another rock step above gains a broad terrace with a fine grey crag ahead - the most dominant feature of the scramble.

The grey crag face-on appears formidable, but the angle is reasonable and the scrambling is easy but airy. The route takes the clean rocks towards the left end of the face. Start on the right side of a triangular slab, then move right and up clean slabs above. The rocks steepen. Go to the base of a small overhang, then traverse right and up - or go left of the overhang, both ways giving good scrambling. The perfect rock continues as a rib to a terrace. The short steep wall above is the most difficult part of the route - climb it straight ahead by a weakness which slants diagonally right. It is awkward to start, with a mantelshelf half-way, to emerge on the ridge top.

There are numerous waves of rock along the intervening ridge, but the next real scrambling is on the summit cone of **The Pike.**

Go right under the base of the rock pyramid to reach the right-hand arête. This slants leftwards to finish on a rock ridge to the summit. There is an easy descent down zig-zag rakes on the right, or you can continue the scramble along the summit ridge down to a grassy col.

After another little hummock descend to the broad col between Crook Crag and Green Crag. The summit can be reached by scrambling up the crags directly ahead, but a far more sporting route is provided by the next scramble which is reached by traversing below the crags. Descend from the col, and walk left below a long line of steep crags, past a grassy break to cleaner more amenable rocks.

Crook Crag, by Great Whinscale

RED SLAB

DETAIL OF
UPPER SECTION

51

GREEN CRAG

51. GREEN CRAG - WEST SIDE   Grade 1/2**   SD 197983

Green Crag is the southerly highest point (1,602ft) of the modest but rocky peaks which rise from the Ulpha moorland. Combined with a scramble on its neighbour, Crook Crag, it gives a fine day's sport. There are crags directly below the summit and a choice of outcrops below. The described route takes a logical line with only short breaks between the crags. Many other ways can be found to suit all tastes.

Approach: As for Crook Crag, past Birkerthwaite to Smallstone Beck which is followed right to the foot of the crags. Aim for the lowest nose of rocks in a direct line with the summit, well right of a steeper band of crag.

Alternatively, after doing the preceding scramble on Crook Crag, descend the westerly slopes from the col before Green Crag to traverse below the steep wall of crags and reach the easier angled outcrops beyond a grassy break.

Character: Excellent rough rock, which is best appreciated in dry conditions. Any difficulties are easily avoided, yet there is plenty of scope for grade 3 scrambling.

The Route: The lowest nose is too steep and dirty to enjoy and is best avoided on its left. Start at the foot of the rib above. Start right along a sloping ledge then climb a rib to a grass terrace backed by a steep low wall. The easiest route is by slabs slanting left to a groove which leads through the steeper rock. Walk across right to the foot of a reddish slab, descending a short rock wall on the way. The right edge of the slab is delightful but beware of a loose block. Walk right again, 100ft, to slabs with a clutch of perched flakes at its foot. Mount the slabs leftwards then move 20ft right to the rib (loose flake). At the top of the knoll, the fine summit crags are revealed.

There is a lot of steep rock, but the right-hand slabs are more practicable and much easier than face-on appearance suggests. They give a fine but exposed finish to the route.

The start lies at the right side at a collection of boulders, where one rests upon another. Another feature is a grass ledge above the start, to the left of the slabs. Climb a blunt nose for 20ft behind the boulders to just below the grass. Cross the steep edge right to gain the rough slabs and a ledge which runs right for 25ft. Climb a slabby rib to a grass terrace. Ascend a steeper rib above then easy slabs to the top.

52. STRAIGHT GILL Grade 3 NY 212009

This is an almost dry, straight cut cleft reached by the pony track from the foot of Hardknott Pass, just 200 yards from the car park. I turned back on this one, but friends assure me that higher up it improves. Low down it is shallow and full of loose scree, but higher it becomes steeper and more enclosed, with three quite steep pitches. The first long pitch is coated with non-slip moss. There is some doubtful rock in the top pitch which is also steep.

53. COWCOVE BECK   Grade 2**   NY 214024

An entertaining, easily accessible scramble, which can provide a sporting trip when poor weather rules out the higher fells. Cowcove Beck drains the boggy moorland shelf between Scafell and Eskdale and joins the Esk half a mile above Brotherilkeld.

In summer bracken encroaches the edges of the gill. There are two impassable pools which detract from the continuity of the route.

Approach: Park 100 yards up the Hardknott Pass road. At the base of the hill take the rough lane towards Brotherilkeld, branching left just before the farm to a path by the river. Cross the footbridge to Taw House and go right along the bridle-path up the valley. After crossing several stiles a stone pack-horse bridge is reached over the beck.

Character: The beck runs in an almost continuous little ravine floored with a solid rock bed which gives top quality scrambling up a series of cascades and pools. The rock is sound and well supplied with positive holds. If you can criss-cross the stream you will enjoy a good scramble, even in poor weather, although the rock is slippery and care is required in such conditions - socks over trainers could be worthwhile. The ravine is low walled with easy escapes almost anywhere. The width of the rock bed allows a good choice of route according to water conditions and in the ascent described was at a medium water level.

Worth saving for a good dry day, yet it can provide a sporting trip when poor weather rules out the higher fells.

The Route: The gill below the bridge is worth scrambling. Go through a gate just past the bridge and descend to the lowest rocks. The first real scrambling is a broad slab with the stream at its left-hand side, and another cascade is surmounted to reach the bridge. Pass under this to the first serious obstacle - a fine narrow, cascade in the back of a dark recess. It is easier than appearances suggest. Start by scrambling up the left-hand side of the first small cascade to a pool. Continue up the slabs on the left of the cascade. At the top of the cascade the slippery exit is almost in the waterchute - if there is too much water escape left a few feet lower and regain the stream above the fall.

Soon the bed narrows into a defile with a slippery traverse on the steep right wall above a deep pool, then pass a conglomeration of fallen trees to another deeper pool with vertical walls backed by a steep fall. This is best avoided by an escape left and regaining the ravine about 100ft above. The next fall is feasible on its right to finish up a central rib with a steep exit.

After passing an opening the ravine begins again, with the first hazard passed on the left wall by a slimy slab, to a sharp bend, then easier going to an ominous cascade above a deep circular pool. Escape left and regain the stream at the head of the cascade. Climb slabs on its left to a break in the gorge. Another broad deep pool lies ahead. Thread through tree branches to reach the left-hand side and traverse just above the pool to a steep climb on good holds near the fall. Cross boulder stepping-stones to the next pool - easiest on the right.

There is easier going for a while always on a broad rock bed. Pass a side gully on the left to a little cascade, climbed on the right. The scrambling continues, always interesting, to a long narrow pool backed by a steep cascade, which can be avoided on its right or climbed close to the fall. Ahead lies yet another cascade with fine slabs on its right to exit on the moor.

To return to the valley join the pack-horse track which lies just to the east. The scramble on Horn Crag provides a logical scrambling route to Scafell.

54. THE ESK GORGE   Grade 2***   NY 227036

Between the junction of Lingcove Beck and the Great Moss, the River Esk runs in a slight gorge of great beauty. A path traverses both its flanks well above the water, but walkers can only glimpse the many falls and pools. The lower end of the gorge opens out and is a very popular bathing and picnic spot on a warm summer day.

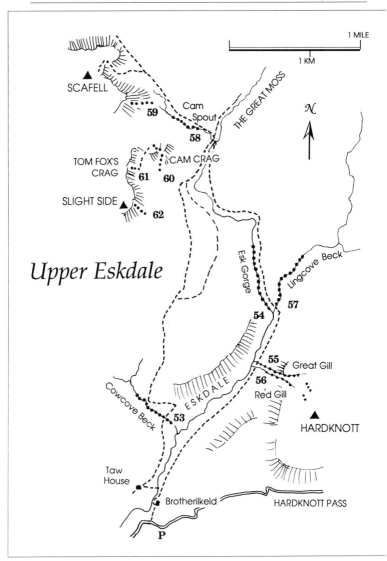

To traverse the bed of the gorge is Lakeland's finest major stream expedition, both sporting and scenic on perfect rock. The river normally carries a strong flow, which runs off slowly, fed by the broad sponge of the Great Moss. If there is too much water it is impossible to traverse round the pool edges and more time is spent out of the gorge than in. Save this trip for a hot day in summer during a prolonged dry spell, when the occasional wade is refreshing.

Approach: Park at the foot of Hardknott Pass, either a few hundred yards above or below the Brotherilkeld lane end. A path bypasses the farm to follow the river for a while, before rising through pasture and up the broad valley to the shapely pack-horse bridge at the confluence with Lingcove Beck.

Character: Perfect rock and deep green pools make an attractive combination in a dry spell. The first section is open and the most interesting way must be sought, but later it develops into a more intimidating ravine where there is no escape for a while. Some of the traverses above deep water seem formidable at first glance, but prove reasonable. There are several places where a short, thigh-deep wade is necessary. Best done on a hot day in shorts and trainers.

The Route: Just above the pack-horse bridge is an impassable pool. Gain the rock bed of the right bank just above the bridge by a grass shelf. The first difficulty is a prow, which is rounded at water level followed by a steep ascent to a ledge. (Or gain the ledge more easily on the right.) Traverse a damp recess, feet in the water and climb close to the fall. This completes the initial cascades and a short walk leads into a verdant ravine and a fine pool, backed by an attractive fall. Go around the left side and ascend the rocks through a narrows to emerge at a broad pool and a 40ft waterfall. The rocks of the right wall make an attractive pitch. Pass the next pool by a ledge on the right and up a steep groove with good holds.

The angle is easy for a while but the broad rock bed provides good sport if you search for it. Make a fun crossing of the stream at a corbel. Cross to the left side of the stream just before the next narrowing. Gain the central rocks and up a groove at the right-hand end of the next steep wall. Cross the stream again with care onto a central block. Cross back right at the lip of a pool to climb a steep flake crack with a small tree. Descend a rib to the exit of a deep pool and up a steep rib on the other side onto grass. Regain the solid rock bed above. A small circular pool is best passed by a thigh-deep wade on its left side. Mount the left rib at the top - or cross to the right and up a flake crack. Climb the left rib of the next pool to open rocks - gain the central rocks. At the end of this is a bold leap across a deep channel and a tricky rising ramp on the block above. At the top cross to the slabby right wall.

The next pool is impassable and is avoided on the right. Regain the bouldery stream bed and cross a fallen tree which has slid into the bed from the side wall. How long it will remain depends on the strength of floods. The ravine becomes deeper and more forbidding, with darker mossier rocks which add to the atmosphere. Easy scrambling along the left side leads to a long deep pool backed by a fall. Traverse the mossy right wall with surprising ease to a more delicate ascent at the side of the fall. Cross the stream left onto a rib. Wade a short pool to gain mossy slabs of the right wall. It is easier for a while to another longer wade along the left side of a steep-walled pool. Climb onto a ledge at its end and follow this above a deep pool, with an awkward little descent. Still on the left wall, the next pool is conquered by a serious traverse of a steep shattered wall, starting with a slight descent from a jutting block onto a rising traverse. Gain a shelf. This traverse proves much easier than first appearance suggests. Traverse slabs to a house-size boulder which blocks the ravine. Climb the short steep crack at its side to end the serious section.

A sting in the tail is provided by the final fall. Traverse mossy rocks on the right edge of a pool. The shelving rocks close to the fall are more difficult than anything else on the trip and most people will paw the rock then retreat a few feet to escape up the flank to end a satisfying expedition.

There is a choice of good scrambling continuations in Upper Eskdale, perhaps the best for climber/scramblers is to take advantage of the low water conditions which allow an ascent of the Esk, to continue up the demanding direct ascent of Cam Spout.

55. GREAT GILL   Grade 2*   NY 227029

This is the best of the minor gills along the side of Eskdale. Although not comparable to the quality of its near neighbours, the Esk Gorge and Lingcove Beck, it makes a novel approach to the humble craggy summit of Hardknott, (1,800ft).

Approach: As for the Esk Gorge - walk up the gentle valley path from Brotherilkeld. The steep right-hand side of the valley has a craggy rim - note the isolated pinnacle, The Eskdale Needle, high up. Well past this is a crag with two gills cutting through the hillside. The left-hand one is the scramble, about half a mile below the pack-horse bridge over Lingcove Beck.

Character: A surprisingly rocky gill which rises in a series of steps and small ravines. Unfortunately the main ravine is impassable. Best done in a dry spell when the rough rock can be utilised to the full. The continuation of the scramble on isolated crags set in a lonely, boggy plateau, is quite worthwhile, on excellent rough rock.

The Route: The gill becomes rocky about 150ft above the valley track. The first feature is a 40ft recess, climbed up the stream to bridge up a mossy exit. Two rough slabs follow with a steep traverse left near the top. Another steep recess is climbed on its left but a more serious obstacle above is best avoided altogether. Easier scrambling leads into a defile, where a cascade is passed by steps on the left. Enter a shady ravine guarded by trees. A long mossy rib ends in a steepening - keep to rocks on the left side, awkward mid-way and steep at the top. This is only feasible in a dry spell.

Climb a slab to below a prominent tree, through a slight ravine into a deeper ravine. This culminates in a steep, slimy runnel and is impassable. Abandon the stream at this point and walk up its edge. Take the highest of two grass rakes across the crags on the left. Near the top of the rake climb the rocks on the right, by a rib on the left of a prominent V-corner. The mountain summit lies over to the right and several attractive craglets can be climbed on the way. The first is a knoll reached across the head of the stream.

Climb the slabs at the right-hand end of the knoll, starting at the foot of a blunt rib. Climb slightly right up rough, clean slabs with plenty of holds to a slight ramp right. A prow above a grass ledge is climbed on its left side. An excellent pitch.

Walk to the next knoll on the right, which has a fine sweep of slabs on its front. Climbers could devise satisfying pitches at various standards but a scrambling route exists on the right where a diagonal rib lies just right of a bilberry groove at the edge of the slabs. Climb the rib right to left, with an exposed step onto smaller continuation ledges, to reach the top of the bilberry chute. Finish up slabs on the right.

Further small outcrops lie between here and the summit over to the right.

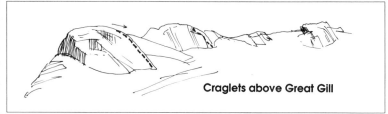

Craglets above Great Gill

56. RED GILL   Grade 3*   NY 225029
Parallel to and very close to Great Gill, this is a deceptive gill which starts as a very easy open stream and becomes progressively more interesting. Similar in quality but quite different to its neighbour.

Approach: 100 yards before Great Gill.

Character: The upper reaches lie in a narrow ravine. Excellent rock interesting situations, quite long.

The Route: After a tame start enter a deep narrow cleft, with a steep short exit. More open streamway follows to a small deep pool at the foot of a band of crags. Above the character of the gill changes.

Traverse round the pool and climb the stepped cascades in the

John Riding starting Mill Gill, Thirlmere in ideal water conditions

The lower part of Galeforth Gill, Longsleddale,
is a continuous rock staircase. Aileen Evans.

Hayeswater Gill, Patterdale. When ice abounds, gill scrambling needs
care! John Riding.

narrow ravine. This is quite easy at first but a steeper 12ft tier proves tricky - best on the drier left side. The gill lays back a short way before steepening again. A second awkward pitch is reached which is taken on mossy rock to the right of the cascade. Watch out for large loose blocks! The gill again flattens and a fork is reached. Take the main streamway on the left and another rift-like passage is entered which contains two more steep mossy pitches leading to the top.

The gill ends in the area of outcrops of sound rough rock described in the previous route. Alternatively a walk right along the rim of the plateau will take you to the Eskdale Needle, a fine pinnacle.

57. LINGCOVE BECK   Grade 2**   NY 227036
An expedition of great beauty best done after a prolonged dry spell. Despite some disjointed scrambling due to impassable falls, it is quite worthwhile if only to enjoy stream scenery at its best.

Approach: Park at the foot of Hardknott Pass in Eskdale, follow the farm lane to Brotherilkeld, where a track leads up the broad flat valley to a pack-horse bridge over Lingcove Beck at its confluence with the Esk. An alternative approach is from the Duddon side of Hardknott - park near the foot of the pass where a path traverses the hillside into Mosedale. Cross a low col at the head of Mosedale and descend the side of Lingcove Beck to the pack-horse bridge.

Character: A fairly narrow, shallow ravine with escapes possible anywhere, with deep pools, short falls and good rock to give interesting sport. The stream drains a major valley and can carry a lot of water.

The Route: Start above the first impassable fall. Traverse awkwardly on the left wall or boldly jump the boulders to gain the pool below another fall to bypass the cascade on its left. Keep left on rocks past the next fall to an attractive diagonal spout into an almost enclosed circular pool. Climb the exposed stepped rib which forms the right edge of the pool to the top. Regain the gill where the stream is split by a central block. Creep round the right edge of the pool to the neck behind the block and make a bold step across the water to gain a rock stairway. This completes the first steep section.

A ravine starts just above and progress is interesting, criss-crossing the stream amongst delightful rock scenery. At a deep pool traverse a mossy shelf on the right wall to reach a jammed block by a fall. Go below the block and straddle the spout. Now there is a slabby right wall above a deep pool. Traverse it delicately for about 20ft to a point where you can ascend mossy rocks onto a traversing line to the top of the three falls. Traverse the next pools on the left and pass a small step by a damp overhung slab. The main scramble ends just above.

Further up the valley towards Bowfell, the stream develops into two more scrambling sections. Highly recommended is the other major scramble in the area - the Esk Gorge, for if the water level is low enough for Lingcove Beck, then the Esk should be in condition.

58, CAM SPOUT   Grade 3 Direct**   Grade 1 Indirect   NY 218058
The stream (How Beck) which descends from below Mickledore and Scafell, tumbles down attractive cascades in a small rocky ravine to the flat grassy area around the Great Moss. A path zig-zags close to the ravine but views into it are limited.

Approach: Cam Spout lies on the main path to Scafell from Eskdale, approached either by the valley route or the higher level shelf on the north-western side of Eskdale. The ideal approach is by the Esk Gorge scramble.

Character: The direct route sticks as close as possible to the bed of the gill and poses some rock climbing problems in exposed situations. Rope advised. The rock is excellent. The main waterfall pitch can only be achieved in dry conditions. The indirect route is a very inferior soft option.

The Route: The indirect route is obvious - close to the right edge with divergence into the stream where the angle eases above the main fall.

The direct scramble starts with a traverse of the first pool and a tricky start to ascend the right wall. Regain the bed of the second pool and ascend the right wall with close views of the main fall. The way merges onto the rocky edge of the ravine which is followed to join the path.

Regain the stream bed at a fine amphitheatre of red rocks down which the stream cascades. Make sure there is not too much water near the top before embarking on this long and serious pitch, which is only for the experienced climber/scrambler. Mount rock steps in the left corner of the cascades, awkward in places, to reach a sloping shelf below a steeper barrier. Go right to cross the water and descend the shelf to gain good holds on the right wall. Climb steeply until the bed can be regained.

Follow a trench on the right of the water, easier now, but still interesting. The angle lessens but the narrow gill gives good sport to open ground in the combe below the rocky south-west side of Scafell - which can provide a continuation scramble almost to the summit ridge.

59. SCAFELL - SOUTH-EAST SIDE   Grade 3*   NY 214061

From the grassy combe above Cam Spout, Scafell appears as a shapely pyramid of jumbled slabby crags. There is a steep crag close to the summit and a continuous broad belt of slabs low down. An interesting scramble with a minimum of walking can be devised, with a choice of routes. The difficulties described could be bypassed.

Approach: A good continuation to Cam Spout. Or walk up the path by Cam Spout into the combe and cross the stream to the lowest rocks just above the path.

Character: Open, slabby scrambling on good rock, quite exposed, serious and difficult in parts. Rope advised.

The Route: The lowest rocks are characterized by an overhung base on the right side. Start at clean slabs to the left of this, left of mossy slabs. At its top walk right to a grass terrace leading right. Climb the first

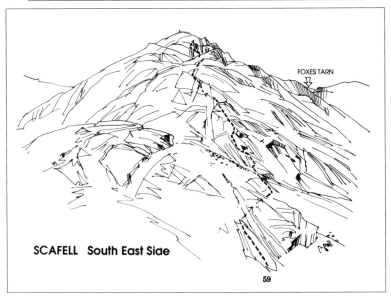

FOXES TARN

SCAFELL South East Side

59

continuous slabs above which lead to a terrace below more imposing slabs ahead, which form a steep and serious section of the route.

There is a prominent overhang in the slabs. Gain a groove directly below this from the left. Climb it until below the first overhung recess, then bear left to the edge. Just round the corner is an exposed gangway which provides a way across a very steep wall. Traverse this to a juniper ledge, and continue up to the left but not too far as this leads off the rock. Move back right to enjoy the superb rough rocks of the buttress front. String the rocky bits together till they end at a junction of gullies. Cross to rocks on the left, and again a little higher, before it peters out. Cross the scree on the right and walk to the steep buttress above.

The buttress provides a difficult finish. Just up the right wall of the steep rocks a gangway slants left above the steep nose. Cross this, exposed, and pull onto easy rocks on the front. The scrambling eases into walking to the broad summit ridge of Scafell.

60. CAM SPOUT CRAG   Grade 1   NY 215055

The route described provides an unusual but toilsome way onto the Scafell ridge. Cam Spout Crag is steep and grassy but a diagonal scree rake makes an obvious line.

Approach: From the path below the crags gain the left-hand side of the rocks.

The Route: Some preliminary mossy rocks can be climbed to gain the start of the diagonal rake. This proves to be of scree, but the toil can be minimised by keeping to the right edge. It ends on the brink of a dramatic overhanging drop into Peregrine Gully, the impressive but loose rift which is a prominent feature of the crag. Scramble up the exposed edge of the buttress above. At a steepening bear left until the edge can be regained. Finish up a shattered ridge.

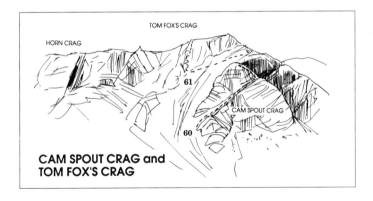

CAM SPOUT CRAG and TOM FOX'S CRAG

61. TOM FOX'S CRAG   Grade 2   NY 212055

This little frequented combe lies above and behind Cam Spout Crag. A cirque of crags rims its edge, above steep screes.

Approach: A special visit would be excessively toilsome, but it provides a logical scrambling continuation to Cam Spout Crag, although it is more serious. From the easy-angled ridge above Cam Spout Crag traverse below the first crag to the left end of the second, to reach a gully amongst slabs.

Character: Lonely and serious, a mountaineering scramble for the competent. The rock needs care.

The Route: Climb a short mossy wall into the gully, then take to rocks on its right. A zig-zag route avoids difficulties, then continue up a fine rock tower which develops into a spiky arête.

The summit of Slight Side lies just to the left.

62. SLIGHT SIDE by HORN CRAG   Grade 2   NY 212048

Slight Side is the southernmost outlier of the Scafell range, rarely visited for its own sake, yet it has a fine rocky summit, a prominent pyramid which commands extensive views. The eastern side of the mountain is the last rampart of the very craggy barrier stretching from above Cam Spout Crag.

The scramble is described with an Upper Eskdale approach as it is a logical continuation to the Esk Gorge, although Cowcove Beck would be an equally good alternative approach.

Approach: From the top of the Esk Gorge bear left up easy-angled grass slopes. A tongue of grass between scree slopes reaches to the lowest crags of Horn Crag which is the prominent buttress directly below the summit.

From Cowcove Beck join the path along the upland shelf to Upper Eskdale. Take the higher path past High Scarth Crag, soon after which Horn Crag is seen on the left.

Character: Solid rough rock scrambling on a broad buttress. Although the scrambling is easy it is exposed with a big crag atmosphere and although the basic rock is good the ledges are strewn with loose stones. Care required.

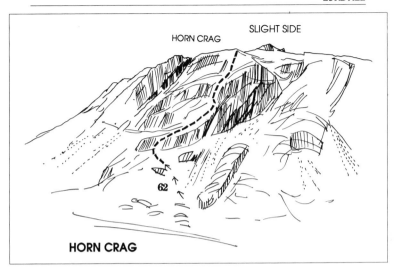

SLIGHT SIDE

HORN CRAG

62

HORN CRAG

The Route: Start at the lowest pink rocks just left of the scree. Scramble into a recess, cross to a spiky rib on the right and go up to a scree shelf. Cross left to another spiky rib, climb it on its left side and continue until it develops into a scree ramp. Do not follow this, but for more interest bear right onto the good rocks of the exposed buttress front. Cross the now grassy ramp to a rock wall. Climb just left of a crack, gain a mossy slab and the edge overlooking the ramp. Continue to a steep wall, climbed on big holds in its centre by a right to left ascent. Scramble by the left side of a cleft to finish.

The top is a few hundred yards further. Finish with a flourish up the summit slabs. A cairned descent path lies to the south of the crags.

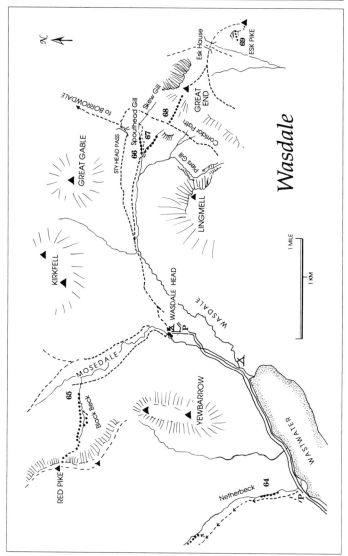

The shapely fells around Wasdale Head attract many visitors, but the major climbing crags are generally too fierce to provide good scrambling routes. Likewise the faulted ravines of the Scafell range attract only to disappoint. Most of the obvious popular routes were described in the first *Scrambles*, but a gap has been filled with the inclusion of a fine craggy route on Red Pike, one of the longest in the Lakes. The Netherbeck Gorges make an interesting filler for a hot day.

There are campsites at Santon Bridge, a well-situated popular site at Strands, the National Trust site at Wasdale Head, and a small site at Wasdale Head Inn.

63. WHITE BAND CRAG, MIDDLEFELL   Grade 2*
NY 147062

Middlefell contains a plethora of rock, much of which can be used for scrambling. Two routes were described in the original *Scrambles*. This route lies well to the left on a prominent buttress towards the western end of Middlefell, the last notable rocks before Greendale Gill.

Approach: Park below the rocks about half-way between Wastwater and Greendale Farm along the Gosforth road. Walk up bracken slopes to the rocks, which have a prominent white quartz band.

Character: Somewhat mossy rock, but firm and rough with a choice of routes. A pleasant exposed outing.

The Route: Start at the lowest subsidiary rocks at a steep nose with a tree on its right. Climb the left side. Walk to the foot of the main rocks where a central depression with two trees is flanked by ribs. The left is easy, the right is steep at first. Avoid the steep start by a rake on the right-hand side. Easy mossy slabs are then climbed to the 20ft high White Band. Cross this and climb slabs above right of centre, just left

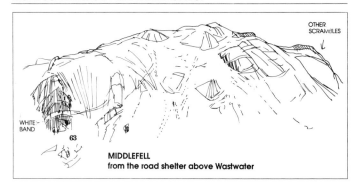

OTHER
SCRAMBLES

WHITE-
BAND

63

MIDDLEFELL
from the road shelter above Wastwater

of a mossy scoop. Level with a tree on the right the angle eases. Climb the centre of rough slabs for 60ft, then take a line diagonally right, crossing below a mossy crack. 20ft round the corner climb the front of a rib for 15ft then move left 15ft into a groove. The easiest line is on the right, linking grassy ledges about 20ft left of the right edge to the top of the rock knoll.

Ahead slightly left are more rocks - walk across to the first slabs, gained by a break in the steep left wall. Pleasant scrambling then leads to the top. Other minor outcrops further right can be incorporated on the way to the summit.

If you descend towards Greendale Gill to the west, you will notice two narrow rocky gills on its eastern side - TONGUE GILLS. The left-hand one is a particularly striking rocky rift with thin waterslides. It is easy to the first fall, but an ascent of the right wall of this would involve difficult rock climbing. Escape up the side is loose and not recommended. The falls above are slimy and again would involve genuine rock climbing. Not worth investigating.

64. THE NETHERBECK GORGES Grade 2* NY 161070
Two gorges in this gently rising valley are of spectacular beauty. Trees almost form a canopy over the gorges and few walkers realise that just below the path is a deep vertical gash with cascades, pools and a fine waterfall.

Approach: Park by Netherbeck Bridge on the side of Wastwater. Walk up a few hundred yards to join the main path, but soon leave it to enter the first gorge.

Character: Quite different to the usual Lakeland gills, for the granite rock is more massive with few holds. The ravine is square-cut, with vertical walls and a very bouldery bed. There are deep pools which cannot be avoided and thigh-deep wades are necessary at times. The atmosphere is verdant and oppressive between the dark beetling walls. Escape is feasible in few places. The scrambling is generally easy, with just an occasional difficulty. Save it for a lazy, hot summer day in a dry spell.

The Route: Walk to the first fall defended by a deep pool. Wade the left side to gain a central rib. The next cascades are climbed by the left wall, starting with an awkward traverse on slippery rocks over a deep pool to reach a central spur. It is easier for a while but leaps across mid-stream boulders maintain the interest. The ravine narrows with steep walls and another wade at the right of a pool. Round a bend the final waterfall comes into view, the crux of the first gorge, and a rope may be useful.

Gain the left side, (possible escape up tree roots here), then traverse a mossy gangway which steepens into an overflow channel. The vertical lip is crossed in an exposed position, with a useful foothold on its edge.

Walk half a mile to the second gorge which is not so beautiful as the first, but perhaps more difficult in its central part.

Enter the gorge by a sheepfold, then bouldery walking to where the ravine narrows between vertical walls. There is a thigh-deep wade in dry conditions, then boulder bed scrambling along the ravine floor. The walls heighten and overhang - slimy pink-tinged rock decked with trees and ferns. Keep right past a small cascade to a deeper pool. This is the crux. Edge thigh-deep around the left wall, then with the aid of underwater footholds gain a shelf just on the left of a small fall. Don't fall in! Awkward. Pass the pool above and climb a steep step.

A tangle of fallen trees adorns the next cascade. Climb the rocks on its right. Another deep pool is crossed on the left then wade into the centre on a submerged rock and right of a large boulder. (There is an escape left above this.) Pass a mid-stream boulder which sprouts trees from its top, then wade a deep pool and climb the right side of huge boulders. Cross the boulders at the top to the left side along a gangway. Cross right above and complete the gorge by easier scrambling.

65. RED PIKE (2,707ft) from BLACK BECK   Grade 2** NY 175102

A vertical height of 1,900 feet makes this one of the longest mountaineering scrambles in the Lake District. Red Pike's Mosedale flank is very craggy and complex. This route, based on Black Beck, explores two craggy combes and ends within a few feet of the summit. In Haskett-Smith's early guide *Climbing in the British Isles* (1894), the rocks of Red Pike are mentioned. It seems as though few people have explored them since, for the combes are trackless and lonely.

Approach: Park at the green triangle at the head of Wasdale and walk to the hotel. Cross the river at a footbridge and follow a path into the flat valley of Mosedale. Pass the worn out scree shoot of Dore Head. Black Beck is the first stream which drains from Red Pike.

Character: A chain of small craglets are linked to make a long mountaineering scramble with a little walking between sections. The whole mountainside is a welter of crags of varying degrees of steepness, which offer scope for much variation. The route described aims to link the cleanest rocks. In the beck the rock is slaty, a little of the crag scrambling is vegetated, but on the whole the rock is rough and sound - a joy to climb. Any difficulties are easily avoided and there is scope for more difficult rock climbing variations if required. Avoid the route in damp conditions when the rock becomes treacherous.

The Route: From the valley floor walk up the bouldery beck which becomes scrambly where it enters a narrowing past a tree. Take the

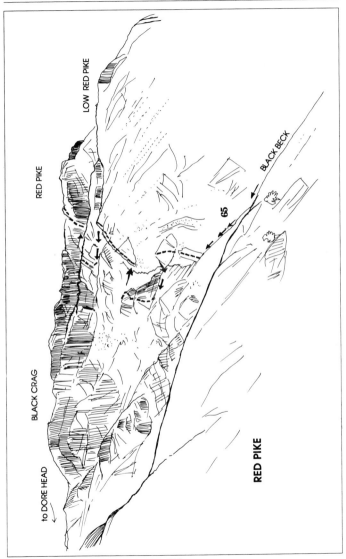

LOW RED PIKE

RED PIKE

BLACK BECK

65

BLACK CRAG

RED PIKE

to DORE HEAD

right fork into a defile where the stream falls over the right wall. Climb the steep wall just left of the stream on good holds to a mossy exit. (The left branch of the stream bypasses this difficult pitch.)

Black Beck issues between crags above, with the cleanest rocks to its right. (Other possible good scrambling lies on crags well left.) Climb the rib, starting a few feet up on the left. Good flake holds lead to a grass ledge with another length of slabby rib above. This is most easily started 15ft up on the right in a corner - step onto the rib and ascend it airily. After a grass ledge the rib continues, move into a groove on the left to finish. Go up rough slabs on the left to exit on grass slopes.

The next good buttress on this side of the stream lies well above, but the crags on the left of the stream, whilst more mossy and vegetated, offer some interest to gain height. Cross the stream and walk to the left-hand end of the lower crag. Move strenuously right onto a large pointed block. Step left from its top and mount slabs. Climb a spiky ridge at the right edge of the next craglet to a mid-point ledge. The rib steepens above but can be flanked by walking right along the ledge, which turns into an exposed slab. Step round a corner - care; some of the foot level blocks are loose - to easy ground. Interest can be maintained by a devious traverse back above the slab onto the front of the buttress.

From the top of the knoll walk across the stream right to the foot of a clean crag of very rough rock. Start up the left end and climb steeply to a grass ledge. From the right end of this climb a steep wall onto rough slabs. A little outcrop on the right gains height to the next long stretch of slabby ribs. More slabs follow to a grass hollow where the best rocks lie well to the left.

Walk along a flat shelf for about 200 yards. Do not go too far where the crags are steep, but aim for a narrow rib of slabs which start above a lower broken tier above the shelf. The lower tier is climbed by steep little walls, then move left to the clean sweep of slabs which emerge on the edge of the summit combe.

Crags ring the combe and it is difficult to choose the best way, for there is a lot of steep rock and much scrappy rock, with no obvious good scrambling route. However, the following proves better than it looks. Directly ahead is a steep crag reached by walking along a marshy shelf. Below the main crags are subsidiary rocks on the left of scree. Start up the rib, then move right to a slab, climbed by a grassy groove on its right. The rock fizzles out into the scree below the main crag. Go directly ahead to a shallow mossy gully. Start up the gully for 20ft then move onto knobbly rocks on the right. Where these run into scrappy ground move right onto exposed slabs with good holds onto the final slopes. Walk right to a small rock block which ends a few feet from the ridge. The summit lies just to the right.

Once on the ridge there are several options. Scoat Fell and Pillar lie close by and a fine round can be made to Black Sail Pass. If you choose to descend from Red Pike by the regular route to Dore Head, be warned - the steep screes into Mosedale used to be a fine run but wore out many years ago. Now it is a dangerous bare slope with a very steep path at its side. A more interesting and very easy descent which explores the northerly craggy combe of Red Pike is as follows. Walk the ridge to the col between Red Pike and Scoat Fell. Turn right down a steep slope then bear left across a shoulder. Keeping diagonally left descend between a band of crags to a broad grassy shelf above the slabs of Elliptical Crag. Drop down the far side of these on grass to easy grass slopes in the valley bottom. This route completes a fine mountain day, but care must be taken to spy out the correct line from the ridge, as descent too early could be dangerous.

THE WASDALE RAVINES

From Great End to Lingmell the Wasdale side of the mountain is riven by several fault-controlled ravines. The largest and most renowned is PIERS GILL, which is a magnificent but severe rock climbing scramble feasible only in drought. The left-hand offshoot of Piers Gill is GRETA GILL, narrow and straight, with nothing for the scrambler, for the initial part is bouldery and impassable waterfalls bar the way above. Left again are two small ravines past Stand Crag - GRAINY GILLS - the right fork does offer some scrambling until it becomes too difficult. The final fault lies in the valley stream itself, SPOUT HEAD GILL, which is well worth incorporating into the day's sport.

66. SPOUT HEAD GILL Grade 2 or 3* NY 214092

Approach: Follow the track along the valley where the main Sty Head path starts to rise. This old pony track makes a very pleasant alternative to the main track. Pass the confluence of Piers Gill to the next confluence.

Character: Good quality rock and interesting stream scenery make this short scramble worthwhile.

The Route: The first real obstacle is a 30ft cascade climbed by a steep spiky rib on the left. A gentle rock bed leads to more risers. The first, by a tree, follows a bypass, the second takes a central rib to finish up the trough of the stream. Past a pool enter a deeper ravine, where a cascade presents a more formidable obstacle by the rocks on its left wall: (Gr.3). Alternatively retreat and climb the left edge of the ravine entrance (Gr.2). Mount easy risers to a fine slabby cascade. Start on the left up a steep damp wall. Cross the spray to the right side of the cascade and finish up its narrow trough. An excellent pitch. Climb a broad barrier at its right. The fault ends where the stream cascades over its steep left wall - make a way up this.

On the right is the old pony track which makes a useful descent to the foot of Grainy Gill.

67. GRAINY GILL Grade 2 NY 215092

Approach: Best done after Spouthead Gill - this is the right-hand stream at the confluence. Two parallel streams run in faults up the hillside; the right-hand one is larger and carries more water.

Character: More mossy and grassy than the preceding, but there are some good pitches and impressive situations, although the route is feasible only half-way up the ravine.

The Route: At first there is easy open scrambling in a succession of small risers above deep little pools. A 30ft waterfall bars access to the main ravine. Climb a rib on the left to regain slabs above the fall.

Climb to another deep cleft capped by a chockstone. A direct ascent seems improbable and retreat from below the chock is awkward on splintered rock. Avoid it and regain the stream at a bend above. The small fall above is sporting with good holds at the top. The deep ravine above is ascended to a spectacular jammed block. Pass this on the left to a ledge, then surmount a bulge onto the top of the block. This may require a helping push. Progress above is barred by a series of impressive falls. Fortunately there is a steep escape possible on the right wall and the route is best ended here.

A steep walk joins the Corridor path.

68. GREAT END FROM THE CORRIDOR PATH
Grade 2*   NY 221088

The steep crags of Great End above Sprinkling Tarn are of no interest to the scrambler, but round the corner towards Wasdale the mountain presents a less steep but extremely rocky face. The crags can be avoided easily by a zig-zag ascent, but if the challenge of a direct ascent is taken, a long scramble of 1,000ft vertical height, can be made, on rock almost all the way from the Corridor Path to the summit at 2,984ft.

Approach: From Sty Head, as easily reached from Borrowdale as Wasdale. Take the path towards Esk Hause. The Corridor Path branches right after a slight ascent, or take a less distinct short cut. Follow the Corridor Path across the crumbly foot of Skew Gill and through a natural rock gateway. About 200 yards past this the path levels. The route starts just above.

Character: Difficult to assess - there is a lot of excellent rough rock, some interesting pitches, much very easy scrambling; yet it is marred by its north-westerly aspect which promotes green patina on the rock. Thus it stays unpleasantly greasy after rain. A good mountaineering exercise. Almost aerial views into Piers Gill are very fine.

The Route: Start at slabs just above the right end of a long low wall of

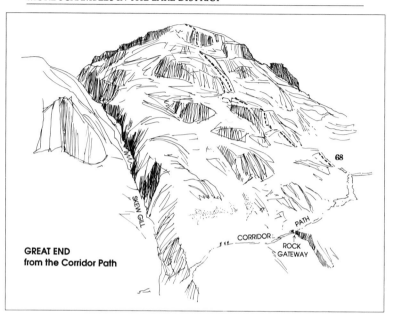

GREAT END
from the Corridor Path

crag about 50ft above the path. Cairn. Climb a grassy groove and the rib on its right. Go left at its top to emerge on a grass terrace below a steep crag. Climb a subsidiary craglet with an overhang, by the easy rocks at its right edge to reach the foot of the steep crag. Straight ahead is a finger stone on the skyline. Start at the mossy groove below this and immediately move left on ledges. Climb easier angled rock just right of the edge. Finish up a recess left of the stone.

Above another grassy slope are the next crags. Go diagonally up left to a knot of rock below the main crag. The front of this is climbed for 50ft. Start by a ledge right into a small groove. Exit left and up to a bilberry ledge. Step left to gain the next ledge with exits left. Care at top with piled blocks.

Directly ahead is a green slabby rib flanked by mossier rocks. This would make a fine pitch if perfectly dry. An easier way is to start about 15ft right, climb to the base of the rib, but escape rightwards on ledges to a recess. Edge left round the base of a block to gain a grass

114

ledge on the slabs, with easy rocks left. Cross boulders to gain a sweep of cracked slabs, climbed at a flake on the right side, difficult at first. Cross a scree gully to better rock on the left.

The bands of crag go on and on, but the angle is now easier and the scrambling undistinguished, over a jumble of blocks and slabs. The rocks are smoother and it is difficult to make a satisfactory route if greasy. Go left to a better rib. Reach a flat grass terrace with a short, steep crag. Climb a right-slanting groove under an overhang, or avoid it right. Continue easily to another terrace. Walk right 30 yards to the base of a short rock pyramid and climb the right edge of this.

The final mossy crags lie ahead. Climb a mossy subsidiary rib to the steep rocks. Go left across a block into a short grass groove. Up this to gain the crest of a rib. Avoid the next part on grass to the right and exit with great care up a corner topped by loose scree. Climb a rib on the right to a grass platform with an overhang. Climb this on the left. Sporting, by a traverse right on the lip of the overhang to climb the flake above. Swing left at top. An easier way goes straight up to this.

A short boulder field leads to a small cairn on the edge of the summit plateau. The main summit lies ahead.

For a scramble on Esk Pike, walk down the boulder-strewn slopes to Esk Hause, where the attractive knot of crag at the head of Eskdale is seen straight ahead.

69. ESK PIKE FORTRESS   Grade 2*   NY 235066

This short steep crag overlooking the head of Eskdale catches the sun and makes a longer scramble than it appears.

Approach: From Esk Hause cross slopes to below the crag. Cross a stable scree shoot to mount steeply to the foot of an easy-angled spur below the steep main crag, which here takes on the aspect of a fortress.

Character: A short scramble with a big crag atmosphere. Good rock.

The Route: Follow the slabby rib, then cross to the next slab right.

Climb the right side of this - care with blocks at top of groove. The various ribs and slabs merge onto a grass rake overlooking the gully. Climb up ledges - zig-zag carefully past a perched block - to where a ledge runs back right across the steep face of the crag. Gain the ledge by a short cleft. Round the corner is a broad bay of broken rocks. Climb the back of the bay. At a shelving mossy step, it is perhaps safer to step left onto a square-cut ledge where progress is easier to the plateau.

The summit lies two craglets away. The scramble has a sporting climax on the final crag. Start at the lowest slabs on the right. Finish up rocks left of a jutting nose.

ESK PIKE Fortress

69

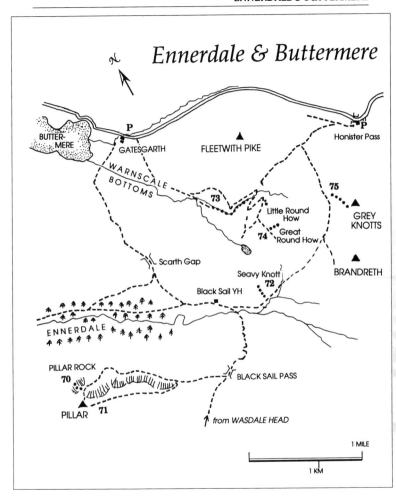

Ennerdale & Buttermere

N

BUTTER-MERE

P

GATESGARTH

FLEETWITH PIKE

Honister Pass

P

WARNSCALE BOTTOMS

73

Little Round How

75

GREY KNOTTS

Great Round How

74

Scarth Gap

Seavy Knott

BRANDRETH

72

Black Sail YH

ENNERDALE

PILLAR ROCK

70

BLACK SAIL PASS

PILLAR

71

from WASDALE HEAD

1 MILE

1 KM

Pillar Rock is the pride of Ennerdale and the goal of many. The Old West is a pilgrimage into the beginnings of rock climbing in Britain. Most people approach from the neighbouring valleys as there are vehicle restrictions in Ennerdale itself. Apart from Pillar Rock, there is not a great deal of scrambling interest in Ennerdale. There is a lot of rock but much is of low quality, especially around the western end of the valley. At the valley head the possibilities improve, but Gable Crag, so often greasy, has been ignored for the purpose of this book. Any scrambling here is very serious, steep and grassy. The Bottle-Shaped Pinnacle Ridge is more of a rock climb than a scramble, despite the impression given in climbing guidebooks.

The Buttermere Valley is similar in possessing a lot of rock but not much in the way of good continuous scrambles. The aspect of its combes encourages growth of grass and moss, whilst the fells north of the valley are composed of Skiddaw Slates, which are rarely solid enough to give safe sport. Grasmoor End is an exception, for the slates here are harder.

There are campsites at Gatesgarth and Buttermere.

70. PILLAR ROCK - THE OLD WEST ROUTE
Grade 3s***   NY 172124

The original way up Pillar Rock makes a great scrambling route, particularly so since the descent is made by the Slab and Notch. Both are similar in difficulty although the Old West has its awkward step, high in an exposed position.

The line of the first ascent up the final rocks of High Man is uncertain, but there is no doubting the courage and boldness of John Atkinson, an Ennerdale cooper, who made the first ascent alone in 1826.

Approach: The walk to Pillar is quite long, around two/three hours -

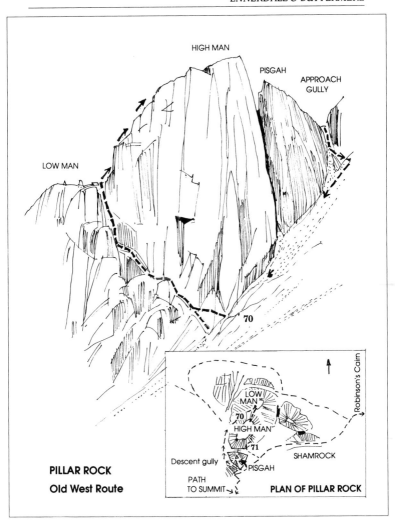

HIGH MAN

PISGAH

APPROACH
GULLY

LOW MAN

70

LOW
MAN

70

HIGH MAN

71

SHAMROCK

Descent gully

Robinson's Cairn

PISGAH

PATH
TO SUMMIT

PILLAR ROCK

Old West Route

PLAN OF PILLAR ROCK

long enough to take advantage of afternoon sun on the west face. The traditional approach is by Mosedale from Wasdale Head. Take the path to Black Sail Pass, or a short cut which branches left on the final slopes; then follow the Climbers' Traverse which undulates across the rocky combes of Pillar's northern flank. At Robinson's Cairn the Rock comes into view. Cross a shallow combe and the path rises. (Note the other track which descends through a gap to the foot of the main face.) Ascend across the top of Shamrock, through a little gap, towards the neck at the top of High Man and Pisgah. Leave your sacks here. (See plan Page 119)

Descend the steep loose gully on the west side of Pisgah where it joins the path on the neck. It soon improves and a slight path is found out left, which zig-zags into the combe below the West Face.

An alternative approach around the foot of Pillar Rock is longer and more arduous. A lot of height is lost to avoid the gully on the right of the Rock. Go well right up a very steep hillside to join a path from Ennerdale which slants into the combe below the West Face. This route gives splendid views of the towering rock and one can fully appreciate the grandeur of the crag.

From Ennerdale - A footbridge almost opposite the Rock gives access to a direct approach.

From Gatesgarth, Buttermere - Cross Scarth Gap Pass and take a right branch which descends through forest to cross the River Liza by the FRCC memorial footbridge.

A scrambling alternative approach is from Mosedale by Wistow Crags (Gr.3), described in the original *Scrambles*. Cross the top of the mountain and descend a steep path, cairn at the top, to the neck above Pillar Rock.

Character: Best appreciated when no one else is on the Rock, when the aura of a big mountain crag oozes from every mossy rock and overhang. I have climbed here on many occasions in the 1950's when the place was swarming with climbers. Today's rock athletes prefer other easily accessible crags. The Old West splits into two sections - a diagonal ascent between steep rock faces to the top of Low Man, then a steeper ascent of walls and terraces to High Man. Best done as a roped scramble to ensure safety in rock climbing situations. The first section is well scratched as it forms the climbers' descent from Low Man.

The Route: There is an obvious diagonal line of weakness which separates the West Face from Low Man. Start at the foot of a light-coloured flare of rock in the centre of the face. This is at the foot of the popular climbs of Rib and Slab, and New West.

Cross a ledge left into a deeper corner and go up diagonally left past the foot of another deep groove capped high up by a huge overhang. Gain a ledge and block on the rib beyond (80ft). Continue along the rising ramp leftwards, cross a sloping slab, slippery if damp, and climb the right edge of a shallow gully for 25ft. Cross left to a ledge and belay spike (100ft).

A path now leads horizontally left to easy ground on the crest. Zig-zag up to a rock tooth and cairn on top of Low Man (230ft).

The rocks of High Man lie above. There is a small spike belay a few feet up the path at the foot of steep rocks. Climb up for 20ft then drop left over a slab and down 20ft to a grass recess - or gain this by a leftwards ascent from the start. Exit left easily onto the base of a ramp. Climb left to the foot of a grass rake.

The ascent continues directly, but it may be worth going up the rake to belay. From the base of the grass rake, climb 20ft to a platform, then move right on shelves for 15ft. The steep ascent above is the crux of the route. Ascend to a perched block and climb the steep cracked wall above. The pull out seems suspect but the block appears firmly wedged. Easier rocks follow to the top. Where you gain the summit, Slab and Notch lies in the deep gully on the left.

71. Descent: SLAB & NOTCH   Grade 3s***

Go down the narrow cleft on the east side of the summit. Where the gully widens, obvious holds cross the slab right (facing out) to reach a ledge with a huge flake block. Descend steeply on good holds to another ledge which leads right to the Notch. Flake belay. A steep descent on the other side of the gap is straightforward if you are tall enough. Cross to the Slab and ascend it to drop off the far side in the gully between High Man and Pisgah. Scramble left to the path and the neck between Pisgah and the mountain, to complete the circuit.

72. SEAVY KNOTT   Grade 3*   NY 203123

An isolated scramble at the secluded head of Ennerdale, above Loft Beck. Not worth a visit for its own sake but pleasantly situated with a sunny aspect and fine views.

Approach: Above Black Sail Hostel, the valley floor is filled with drumlins. Seavy Knott is a crag amongst steep heather overlooking the drumlins. The Coast-to-Coast path rises up Loft Beck immediately below. From this, slant diagonally left to the lowest outcrop with a tree.

Character: Better than it looks; definite holds, rough textured rock, but the crag is serious and contains many loose blocks. A rope should be used for safety but care should be taken to avoid flicking off stones. The described line purposely takes a zig-zag course.

The Route: The first outcrop has a small tree. Either climb the steep difficult rib on the right, or the easy slab 20ft left. Above is a steep broken wall with a tiny sapling at its foot. Go slightly right from the tree to a ledge at 20ft. From the right end of this climb just left of the edge then cross right over heather to belay. Climb a rib above then bear left below overhangs to a good spike belay block on easy-angled rock. (This point can be gained more directly by a route from the middle of the starting ledge.)

Go rightwards to a slab which leads diagonally right to a small block belay below the right edge of the bulging headwall. Climb a ramp at the base of the steep wall, diagonally right to a sapling. Move left onto a ledge and up the steep wall by its right edge. Move left onto the buttress front, then easy rocks to the top.

73. WARNSCALE BECK   Grade 1 with some avoidable 2*
NY 200136

Warnscale Head is steep and craggy. There are pony tracks on either side of the stream, that on the left being the most obvious. The stream itself gives an open scramble with a vertical height of 1,000 feet. Much of the scrambling is easy, on good rock with escape possible almost anywhere. The stream drains a wet hollow and needs to be reasonably low water to make it worthwhile.

Approach: From the car park at Gatesgarth go towards Honister Pass a few yards to where a track branches right into Warnscale Bottoms. Almost level walking gives time to look around at the heathery crags of Haystacks and Striddle, with Green Crag guarding the valley head. It will never be a popular place for climbing, it is far too vegetated and the steep long approaches deter the modern cragsman. Our modest scramble can be seen straight ahead, a stream which bounces merrily over its host rocks.

Character: Not at all serious, yet there are a few places which pose food for thought. Good rock, but like all in this area, slippery when wet. Best in fairly low water when the dry rock can be utilised to the full.

The Route: Start at the first small cascade, topped by a dark green pool. Cross water sculpted rock of the stream bed to a longer cascade with rock slabs on its right. Near its top you can continue up the easy slabs or make a more sporting step across the flow to a steeper finish. The stream bends sharp left into a defile, best passed easily by the rocks on the left. Regain the narrow stream above, duck under a tree and the defile bends sharp right. Cross the slabby right wall by a ledge which peters out. The easiest way is then to step onto a ledge in the water flow and make a few damp moves to reach the lip of the cascade. If there is too much water for this, then the slab is traversed at a higher level with just one delicate step when the holds run out! The right wall is then followed more easily until it opens out.

Above is a broad rock band with the main fall straight ahead. The best scrambling lies near the subsidiary flow to the left, and is reached by a slight descent across the stream. The broad sweep of slabs can be climbed at a rib left of the flow. It steepens near the top, move left (Gr.2). Note the U-shaped groove on its right, gouged by the crampons of ice climbers. This makes an entertaining ascent if you are looking for difficulties. If neither of these routes suit, there is plenty of easier rock.

Just before the streams merge there is a square-cut recess, passed on the right edge. Continue easily on the left side of the stream to a pool and cascade passed most easily on the right. There is bouldery walking now where the stream bends left in a broad ravine. The stream of Green Gully enters on the right. Continue with scrambling here and there. Improving scrambling leads past small cascades - cross to the left wall. There is easier going as the ravine dwindles, then an awkward passage of the left wall, to a walking finish past the final fall.

The main pony track lies just to the left. Another track joins here and a few yards down it on the right, is the tiny bothy of Warnscale Head, a renovated quarry hut.

More scrambling lies ahead on the rock outcrops around Dubs Bottom. Continue along the main pony track to a grassy hollow in front of quarry spoil heaps. A track goes right to cross the stream and goes below the rock prow of **Little Round How** (NY 207132). The rib of the prow can be ascended to its spiny top and the path regained.

Directly ahead is big brother, the fort-like wall of **Great Round How.**

74. GREAT ROUND HOW   Grade 2   (NY 206129)

Pleasant exposed scrambling on good rock, which ends all too soon. The route makes length by following a prominent traversing ledge, tricky to gain.

At the right side of the How is a band of clean light-coloured rock, with a cairn at its foot (marking the start of a slight rock climb), and left of a vegetated slabby recess. Start at the foot of the recess and slant up left to a ledge with a steep exit up a corner. More easily again, the route ascends diagonally left to gain a heather ledge. Follow this left and descend slightly to gain a rock shelf, which is crossed easily in an exposed situation to finish up mossy rocks.

GREAT ROUND HOW

75. GREY KNOTTS   Grade 1   NY 216127

A slight scramble on excellent rock which makes an appetiser to the main fare of the day. The rocks are on the north-west slopes of the hill. It is an interesting alternative to the path.

Approach: Park at Honister Pass.Take the Great Gable path which forks left from the quarry road close to the start. After mounting the steep incline a cairned track goes left over the moor to rise gently across the slopes of Grey Knotts. A line of small crags lie just above the path.

Character: Easy-angled, not serious, scrambling.

The Route: Start at a prominent slabby rib just above the path with its multitude of cairns. Climb the right side then the edge of the rib which steepens a little at the top. Ahead is a slab. Climb slightly right into a small V-groove. Walk right 20ft to a rib. From the base of this, step right onto a shelf to easy ground and ascend to a cairn.

Another craglet capped by a cairn lies ahead. Climb the right side of this. A third cairn crowns a craggy top over to the right. Walk towards this and descend a rake below the steep lowest crag. At the right end is a slabby rib. Climb the front of this, onto a ledge then up the right edge to move left into a niche. Exit right onto easier ground and the summit rocks.

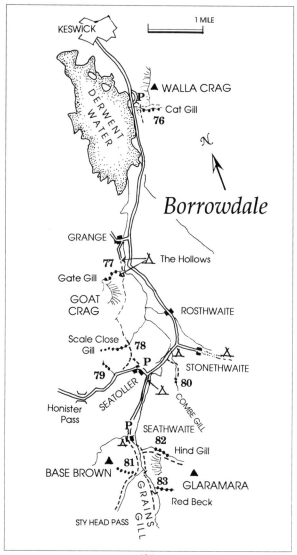

KESWICK

1 MILE

▲ WALLA CRAG

P

DERWENT WATER

Cat Gill

76

N

Borrowdale

GRANGE

⌂ The Hollows

77

Gate Gill

GOAT CRAG

◆ ROSTHWAITE

Scale Close Gill

78

P

79

⌂ STONETHWAITE

⌂

80

Honister Pass

SEATOLLER

COMBE GILL

P

SEATHWAITE

⌂

82

Hind Gill

▲ **81**

BASE BROWN

GRAINS GILL

83

▲ GLARAMARA

Red Beck

STY HEAD PASS

Ease of accessibility and wealth of accommodation make Borrowdale a justly popular centre for climbing, walking and scrambling. There is something to suit all weather conditions, and routes in the neighbouring valleys or fells are easily reached.

Rock quality varies in Borrowdale. In places it is equal to the best of the southern Lakes, in others it is much more friable and smoother. Some of the gills described are very attractive, whilst Jim Riley's long scramble up Base Brown makes an entertaining way to the tops.

There are campsites at The Hollows (Grange), Rosthwaite, Stonethwaite, Seatoller and Seathwaite.

76. CAT GILL Grade 1** NY 272210

Less than two miles south of Keswick, Walla Crag is the first of the rocky, forested bastions which so characterize the eastern bounds of Derwentwater. Completely hidden from view is a delightful gill which curls around the southern edge of the wooded hillside. It is a popular geological excursion, where the succession of rock beds are well seen.

Approach: From the National Trust Great Wood car park in the woods below Walla Crag, take the path signed 'Ashness Bridge' to a footbridge at the base of the gill.

Character: A good long scramble - 600 feet vertical height - in beautiful surroundings, up a narrow rocky gill which catches the afternoon sun. The rock is sound and not too slippery. The water catchment area is not large and so the trip is feasible fairly quickly after rain has run off. A path lies close to the gill and escape is possible at all times. Seek the most interesting rock close to the water for best sport.

The Route: The gill is interesting right from the start, a pretty, narrow little rock trench with scrambling-walking. Climb a little fall to cross the path, then traverse a rock shelf on the right wall. An awkward exit is best achieved by crouching low. An ancient footpath comes close to the gill but ignore this and stick with the rocky bed past a narrow fall, quite awkward to negotiate on its right and exit onto a fallen tree. The gill bends to the left, with some steep little steps to surmount, then narrows into a V-trench with a slabby left wall. Interest is maintained with traverses across little pools and innocent looking but awkward ascents which could be quite wetting if there is too much water flow. A change of character follows with more open rock steps to a final steep wall. Exit on the left with the aid of a fallen pine, or if there is not much water in the gill, the steep left wall can be ascended athletically by a quartz band. After two more short steps the gill emerges onto the moor.

The summit of Walla Crag lies a short way to the north-east, a fine viewpoint. The return path by the side of the gill is well graded and provides an easy descent.

77. GATE GILL   Grade 2/3***   NY 247167
An entertaining trip up the watercourse between Goat Crag and Nitting Haws. The vertical height is 800 feet.
Gate Gill is unnamed on the O.S. maps but has been known by that name locally for generations. The local name for Goat Crag is 'Gate Crag.'

Approach: From Grange take the rough lane towards Hollows Farm. Keep left at a fork to enter the riverside woods and the delectable campsite of The Hollows. The main rectangular camping field on the right has a stile at its top which gives access to the fell. Mount a steep path which bears left to join the stream just above the woods.

Character: This gill carries a lot of water in spate and dwindles to a trickle in a dry spell. There is a solid slabby rock bed for much of the way, but the smooth rock is slippery when wet. Socks over trainers

Aileen Evans climbs the almost dry waterfall pitch in Guerness Gill, Mardale. Some people prefer to scramble in trainers, particularly useful with socks over them in a greasy gill - but they are no substitute for boots

could be useful in greasy conditions and a rope is handy to safeguard the key sections - or effect a rescue if necessary! The scrambling is varied and continuous and culminates in a striking ravine in good situations.

The Route: Start at a tree-lined defile and mount an overhanging block by the stream. On the right wall is a broad slab over which the stream cascades in ribbons. Start at the bottom right and go diagonally left across the water to a small tree. Follow slabs through a V-shaped channel to a boiler plate slab on easy ground.

Walk to the next interest where the stream cascades over a series of stepped slabs climbed on their drier right. Pass a fallen tree to enter a wet recess and climb the middle of this, through a second wet opening. The excellent scrambling continues - go below a holly and climb the steep wall just on its left. A chaos of large boulders leads into a verdant defile between steep walls, where the way is blocked by an unclimbable cascade over smooth rocks.

A way is possible up the mossy rocks on the right (Gr.3). Start up a very slippery slab, where knees prove useful, to reach a tree. A groove slants left above, with good holds over its right edge. There is an easy alternative to this pitch by a grassy ramp on the left.

Regain the stream immediately and climb a crack just right of the water. A stretch of boulder scrambling ends at a large block with mossy slabs on the right. Climb these past the block.

The ravine becomes very impressive where a branch stream enters in a thin fall down the almost vertical right wall. Continue up the main stream ravine, by a steep central rib which curls up to a tree below a smooth cascade. Cross an exposed ramp 20 feet right, then work back left on good ledges to the top of the fall.

The next cascade presents a serious obstacle in all but bone dry conditions, but is easily bypassed on the left. Pass a short steep barrier and cross left to below an overhanging side wall where flakes lead right into the base of a cascade which fills a black cleft. This presents a fitting climax (Gr.3) to a grand scramble. (If there is too much water,

---

Brian Evans climbs the entry to Hopgill Beck, Mardale - in socks over trainers to combat slippery rock. Photo: A Evans

The central slabby section of Gate Gill

escape right through juniper bushes to easy ground.)

The cleft is very wet and about 60ft high. Climb the first section by holds on the right wall until one can bridge to reach a spray-filled platform. The final fall necessitates a steep ascent hampered by the water. *Note there are no belays on this pitch - it needs a steady leader and a rope for the rest of the party.*

There is a little more scrambling - pass an unclimbable fall by ledges on the right wall, then climb a broken cascade. The stream flattens out in a craggy basin below High Spy and several rock outcrops can provide amusement if you are heading for the tops. There is a steep descent path close to the gill.

78. SCALECLOSE GILL   Grade 1/2**   NY 243146

The slopes of High Scawdel are not easily noticed by the traveller in Borrowdale. They lie hidden from the casual glance, behind wooded lower knolls and only a keen eye sees the deep-cut narrow gill biting into a craggy hillside.

Approach: Shortest approach is from the car park at Seatoller, although the path from Grange, behind Castle Crag, also leads to the gill.

From Seatoller cross the stile at the end of the car park and strike directly up the hill to reach the old pony track. Zig-zag upwards on this, but where it heads towards Honister cut right to a gate on the open fell. Follow the path right, over a low col and continue to a footbridge over the gill.

Character: Good rock, interesting scrambling and a vertical height of 700ft make this a first class scramble. The steep parts are short - about 10 to 15 feet, although some steps are quite tricky in places. The water run-off is quite rapid, although in less than a dry spell you can expect to get your legs wet at least, where footholds in the watercourse need to be used.

The Route: Gain the gill above a wall. A black waterslide above a little pool hints at things to come. As usual in this type of scramble, keep close to the water for the best sport - you can easily miss the good bits. There are several little slabby cascades, one capped by a stone, passed sportingly on the left with arboreal assistance. There is a succession of rock steps as the stream passes the first crags, then a change of character - a narrow defile guarded by a fallen tree. Creep under the tree, straddle the pool and make a damp ascent of the narrows - good scrambling! It continues with interest; cross a wire fence and mount steep little rock steps in the gill bed.

The angle relents as the side walls open, but the walls soon close in and the scramble again becomes full of character. I had to fight through a washed down yew tree with a large blue, plastic container trapped in the pool behind. I wonder how long it will stay there? The fall is awkward to surmount on the right and leads to another tricky step, passed direct using the left wall. Round a bend there is a narrow cascade which may be passable in dry conditions. Avoid it by a side channel on the right and regain the gill above. The difficulties are not over yet. There is an awkward two-step rock band which demands neat footwork near the stream and finally another narrow defile before the moor is reached.

There is a straightforward descent near the gill on its south side, or cross the moor to reach the scrambles at the head of the Newlands Valley.

79. HIGH SCAWDELL GILL   Grade 1 or 2*   NY 237142
A pleasant scramble up a short, narrow, rocky gill on the slopes of High Scawdell above the Honister Pass road. It makes an entertaining diversion to fill an odd hour, as it is so accessible, faces south and is on excellent rock. This is one of several gills in the area first ascended by A.R. Thompson and Angelo Dibona in the 1920's. Thompson, who lived in Keswick, was a keen gill scrambler and sometimes, as in this case, was accompanied by his Alpine guide.

Approach: There are parking places on the roadside where the gradient eases after the stiff pull out of Seatoller. The gill is seen on the right above the intake wall. It cuts a small ravine through crags in its upper part.

Character: Clean rock in a narrow bed, with cascades, chutes and many small steps to surmount.

The Route: The way is obvious, the two major difficulties, climbable in dry conditions, can both be easily bypassed on the left.

80. COMB GILL WATERFALL   Grade 2   NY 252133
An alternative route into Comb Gill can incorporate this little scramble - it is worthwhile to see the old corn mill and the waterfall, even if the flow does not allow a scramble. Only feasible after a dry spell.

Approach: Park on the side of the lane to Thornythwaite. Gain the main road at Mountain View and a few yards towards Rosthwaite take a path signed through the fields on the right. Cross the stream at a bridge, turn right and follow the lane to the old mill, which used to grind the corn for the valley. The building has been restored and an old millstone has been incorporated into steps. The iron and timber water-wheel still stands. Continue by the side of the stream to the falls.

Character: A short, steep ascent of a very scenic waterfall. The stream has a broad catchment area and can take a while to subside after rain.

The Route: Scramble into a recess below the steep rock band. The main channel lies on the left and is usually occupied. A lesser spout drops over the vertical wall on the right and if this is only a trickle, the scramble can be made. Go right, round the base of a mossy wall into the area of spray-washed rocks. Ascend damply into a steep groove left of the waterspout, to the top.

81. BASE BROWN from TAYLOR GILL FORCE
Grade 2 or 3** NY 230110

A scramble of over 1,000ft vertical height, which wends a way up a craggy hillside with a sting in the tail. There are fine views down Borrowdale and over Sty Head.

Approach: Park at Seathwaite. Take the path right at the farm, under the arch, to cross the stream. Follow a boggy track up the valley towards Taylor Gill Force. Where the waterfall comes into view, the main path crosses the crag to a gate. Below this are slabs. Descend from the path to the foot of the slabs.

Character: After a steep start the route is open to variation, but a rock band which guards the top makes a fine finish. It is very easy to stray into difficulties, although climbers will relish the opportunities for more difficult direct pitches up the ribs of the higher crags. The rock is generally very sound although mossy in places. On the exposed sections a rope is advised. There is some walking between crags.

The Route: Climb the lowest rocks 30ft right of a holly. At the level of the tree traverse left below a block to a grass ledge. The rocks ahead are mossy and more difficult and are best avoided on the right to reach the path.

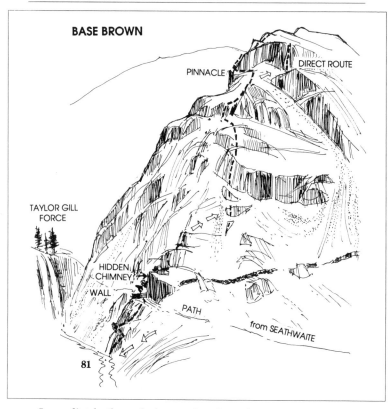

BASE BROWN

DIRECT ROUTE

PINNACLE

TAYLOR GILL
FORCE

HIDDEN
CHIMNEY

WALL

PATH

from SEATHWAITE

81

Immediately through the gate is a deep chimney-groove. This is steep but has good holds and a nut runner can be arranged at the crucial exit. From the ledge above mount a steep wall onto easier angled rocks at the top of the first section.

There is now a wide choice, and the following is a recommended route. Take the bouldery nose on the right. Walk to the foot of prominent rocks above. Climb the left flank of the spur on good holds, moving right at the top. The next steep little barrier is composed of loose blocks. Care! Climb the left end, then zig-zag up.

Ahead is a more serious obstacle - a buttress of steep rock which offers scope for direct rock climbing pitches. The easy way avoids the steep lower rocks by walking left past a juniper patch and up a grassy gully until easy slabs are accessible to the right. Climb these rightwards to the top of a knoll.

Another crag barrier lies above and the easiest route is not obvious. Climbers can make a direct way up the clean spur straight ahead, which steepens at its top, but the easier way described is full of character.

On the left is a pinnacle at the foot of a skyline ridge. Walk to gain a ledge which runs above the pinnacle. Just before the edge belay on a small tree. Climb up past the tree and across a nasty, earthy, heathery scoop to a ledge on the exposed rib. Climb it, bearing left to a large shelf.

The difficulties are now over as easier rocks lead to the top of the spur. The summit of Base Brown is still a plod ahead.

82. HIND GILL Grade 1 or 2 NY 238116

The steep western slopes of Glaramara host several rocky streams. Hind Gill lies close to Seathwaite just north of Hind Crag. A very steep path runs by the side of the ravine, a popular descent from the tops.

Approach: Park at Seathwaite, take the main valley path for quarter of a mile to below the gill where a gate gives access to the fell. The path is faint - zig-zag to the intake gate and drop left into the base of a ravine.

Character: The north-west aspect of the ravine excludes most sunlight and encourages mossy rocks. In poor conditions the rock is slippery and the grade quickly becomes 2 with more than a trickle of water. The gill is long - over 1,100ft vertical height, but the scrambling is limited to the lower half. Much of the trip is over boulders and is lacking in character. Nevertheless it provides a novel way to the tops.

The Route: The ravine rises in mossy steps. Pass a triangular prow on either side to a more sustained section which ends in a tricky ascent of a steep slab. If the water is low, footholds in the stream ease the exit, if high it is much more awkward. After a bouldery section the ravine bed becomes more solid for a while, but soon degenerates into boulder walking. A final mossy defile is impassable and the gill is abandoned for the steep grassy spur on its left.

83. RED BECK   Grade 3s   NY 237103

A fault-controlled gill on the steep slopes of Glaramara above Grains Gill, 2 km from Seathwaite.

Approach: From Seathwaite take the path up the valley, cross Stockley Bridge, continue left up the valley and leave the main path to cross a footbridge over Grains Gill. (The ravine below the footbridge is only accessible at very low water and proves difficult just below the bridge.) Zig-zag up the steep hillside to the start of a small ravine in Red Beck.

Character: One for the connoisseur - interesting if you have the judgement to safely overcome friable rock and steep grass. The side walls of this picturesque narrow gill are brecciated and thus inherently shattered. Note that the same fault line, NW-SE, so typical of the Lake District, can be seen opposite on Base Brown. There are five steep cascades before the gill fizzles out into boulders. Rope advised. The gill is only feasible in a dry spell.

The Route: The first difficulty is a 40ft cascade which is climbed on greasy rock on its left. The ravine bends to reveal a steep fall, the base of which is reached by a rib just to the right of a chute. The left corner of the fall may be possible, but the rock is composed of unsound flakes. Flank the fall by the loose groove on its right to a point where the hanging gardens of steep grass and butterwort can be crossed left to the top of the pitch.

The short fall above is climbed either on its left with a vertical grass finish, or avoided by an earthy diagonal ascent on the right. The cascade above, ending in a large block, is only feasible in dry conditions straight up the watery bed. The final fall is passed on its grassy left by courtesy of a small birch - there is a useful root at 15ft then the tree aids progress to a nasty finish.

The scrambling is now over and a torrent of boulders stretches relentlessly into the distance. Perhaps it is best to take the first escape route out left.

GRAINS GILL AND ALLEN CRAGS

This scramble - No.87 described in the original *Scrambles* mentioned a 'difficult and unpleasant ravine' below the crags. It is reported that in dry conditions the ascent of the ravine is well worth incorporating into the route.

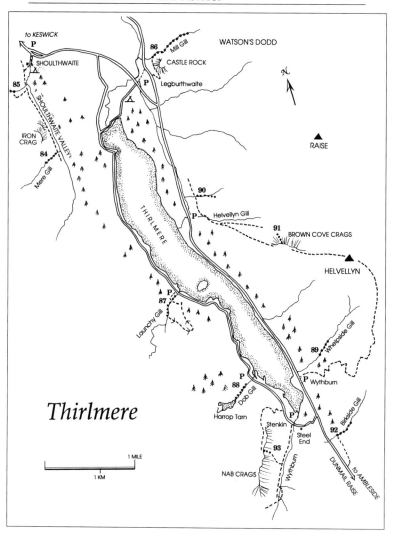

to KESWICK

P

SHOULTHWAITE

85

SHOULTHWAITE VALLEY

IRON
CRAG

84

Mere Gill

86   Mill Gill

WATSON'S DODD

CASTLE ROCK

Legburthwaite

P

N

RAISE

THIRLMERE

90

P   Helvellyn Gill

91   BROWN COVE CRAGS

HELVELLYN

P
87

Launchy Gill

89   Whelpside Gill

P   Wythburn

88   Dob Gill

P

Harrop Tarn

Thirlmere

Stenkin

P

Steel
End

92

93

NAB CRAGS

Wythburn

DUNMAIL RAISE

Birkside Gill

to AMBLESIDE

1 MILE

1 KM

The routes described here enhance Thirlmere's reputation as one of the best scrambling areas in the Lake District. The exclusion of Mill Gill from the last guide drew howls of protest from aficionados, whilst the comment that the western side of the valley was 'too densely forested to offer much in the way of scrambling' was proved wrong almost immediately after publication with the ascent of Launchy Gill. Both these gills should be high on your list of dry spell priorities.

There is a marked difference between the sandpaper-like rock of the western side of Thirlmere, and the silken smooth rock of the east, a practical example of the effects of the north-south fault which bisects Lakeland.

There are campsites at Shoulthwaite, High Bridgend and sometimes at the King's Head.

84. MERE GILL, SHOULTHWAITE   Grade 2+**   NY 298188
The Shoulthwaite Valley is one of those quiet little Lakeland gems bypassed by the majority of walkers. It leads to nowhere in particular and though there are imposing crags, the rock attracts few climbers. Blaeberry Fell must be one of the least visited summits in the Lakes. The excursion described is quite entertaining and can be followed by a stroll along an upland shelf above Iron Crag with grandstand views of the full length of The Dodds to Helvellyn, which from this angle appears to possess a graceful summit cone.

Approach: The Shoulthwaite Valley lies behind the forested slopes above the northern end of Thirlmere and is approached via Shoulthwaite Farm. A private lane leaves the main A591 opposite a loop of old road which is now reserved for parking although there is a 2 hour limit. There is room for parking at the end of the farm lane, but permission is required. Shoulthwaite is an attractive sheltered camping and caravan site.

A signed permissive path goes up the field by the stream to cross a stile and join the right of way path up the valley. Walk well past the beetling Iron Crag to reach Mere Gill which is an unmistakable rocky defile.

Character: If this gill is not bone dry, it must be ascended in socks; for the rock although rough, is slippery, especially where it is black. The only feasible solution is to use trainers with socks over the top, when the holds are transformed from impossibly slippery to very reasonable. In boots the route would be foolhardy.

The gill is a succession of interesting scrambling problems in scenic situations. Whilst the difficulties are short, the general nature of the scramble puts it at the top of its grade. A rope could be useful in places for those unfamiliar with scrambling in socks.

The Route: There is an introductory section below where the path crosses the gill. To do this go down the path to enter a ravine in the main stream. Above the path there is a delicate move almost straight away, on the left wall. A tree root proves a welcome hold, then step into the watercourse.

The black cascade above is steep and slippery. Cross the pool at its foot and keep close under the bulging wall on the right of the cascade until forced to ascend steeply on good holds. Above, climb rocks near the left edge with a steeper finish onto an opening in the ravine.

Another ravine beckons ahead. Mount the first waterslide slabs on the left, quite tricky, then cross right into the ravine. Ascend the right wall by a gangway. The good scrambling continues - a steep wall is ascended, then easier rocks to a pool passed on the right under trees.

It is worth continuing up the narrower defile ahead, which gives sporting scrambling to a final steep wall.

The scramble in Goat Crag Gill can be reached by walking along the shelf above Iron Crag to reach a descending rake below Goat Crag. There are traces of an ancient pony track here. The gill to the north of Iron Crag, which appears a possible scramble in its upper part, is not worth a visit.

85. GOAT CRAG GILL   Grade 2   NY 293202

This short scramble lies up the first gill on the right as the flat valley floor is gained after ascending the path from Shoulthwaite.

Approach: Cross a stile and turn right by the side of a wall. Shortly after the wall bends right, go through a gate and mount steep bracken-covered slopes to the foot of the ravine.

Character: Similar rock to Mere Gill and the same remarks apply. Definitely for socks over trainers, although there are no real difficulties.

The Route: Little rock steps enter an arboreal defile which develops into good scrambling on the slabby right wall. Little slabby steps continue to below a fringe of water over a black overhang. Keep on the slabs on the right.

86. MILL GILL, ST. JOHN'S VALE   Grade 3s***   NY 321198

Tucked into the steep hillside behind Castle Rock is this superb gill, one of the best in the Lake District and a justly popular outing. Put it high on the list of priorities for a dry spell.

Approach: Park at the Legburthwaite car park a short way along the St. John's Vale lane from Stanah on the A591. Follow the path marked Castle Rock, cross the road and a stile, turn right on a track which circles leftwards. Go through a stile at the wood corner and over the leat into the woods directly below the main crag. A path left crosses the wall and keeps just above the wood into the gill.

Character: A splendid succession of incidents in a rocky ravine with a vertical height of 600 feet. To enjoy the expedition you need a dry period. The entry pitch soon becomes impossible and other pitches would be unpleasantly hazardous in all but low water. In a dry spell all the falls except one are feasible direct. Some of the wet mossy rock is slippery and a popular solution is to use trainers with socks over the top where necessary. A rope is necessary to safeguard several steep pitches.

The Route: Enter the dark verdant recesses of the narrow ravine to climb the right side of a short fall. If you can surmount this dry, then the route should be feasible. Not far ahead is an unclimbable fall clenched between steep, smooth, rocky walls. Exit on the right, a series of steps and ledges. Regain the bed of the gill easily at the top of the fall. The next mossy cascade is bypassed on the right wall using tree roots for assistance. Cross the slippery rocks at the top of the cascade and continue in a rock trough to a widening.

A deep pool is passed on its left. Ignore the right-hand branch of the gill and keep in the main stream which swings left and eases in angle. By keeping to the rocks of its left wall a sporting traverse ends in a long stride onto a perched block. A quieter section follows where the gill cuts through the easier angled slopes level with the top of Castle Rock.

The walls close in as the next ravine is entered and easy scrambling past several small cascades leads to a deep little pool defended by steep walls. Either make a tricky traverse of the left wall, or wade into the pool until it is possible to bridge up the cascade at its back. Ahead, a waterfall shoots over a broad steep barrier. Reach its foot by slabs on the right wall, then climb a central rib to the barrier. Cross the right-hand flow to climb the steep right wall on good holds.

The good scrambling goes on and on in a succession of little cascades and falls. Enter a narrowing awkwardly and bridge damply up the next fall. Keep on the right wall past the next fall, with a steep, awkward, exposed little wall at the top, to reach an arched block. You can pass this on its left or do a caving through route.

The most continuous scrambling is now over but it is worth continuing as interesting hazards still appear. There is a steep tricky cascade - start on the left then step across to ascend the right wall. The next fall is rounded on the left. Another cascade by the left side of a huge jutting block is climbed on its left entered by a delicate traverse. Or avoid it by climbing much higher. The rocks to the right of the fall are insecure blocks. The next cascade has slabs on the left and nettles to finish.

Still it goes on ... a cascade over green mossy rock - start on the left and go behind a detached block to gain slabs above. The gill appears to be finished, yet there is a tricky traverse of a right wall and an ascent of two cascades before it finally fizzles out.

87. LAUNCHY GILL   Grade 3***   NY 299158

Hidden amongst the dense forest which clothes the western side of Thirlmere is this delightful gill, one of the most continuously interesting scrambles in the Lake District and also one of the most accessible. A vertical height of around 600 feet gives a good long scramble. A nature trail crosses the gill, above which the upper ravine penetrates difficult craggy terrain which enhances the feel of adventure.

Approach: There is a parking place along the road not far from the foot of the gill.

Character: Full of character, especially if the trip is done as described. Excellent rough rock, verdant gorge scenery. Best in low water during summer. Too much water renders the best bits impossible.

The Route: The interest begins just above the road, where a fault at right angles to the main stream causes the water to flow in a narrow defile. Traverse the steep left wall, just above the water level. At the next bend climb the left wall of a small cascade, awkward to start. A more open easier section remains sporty if the chosen route keeps close to the water. There is an overhung pool and spout to surmount before a mass of huge boulders lead to the footbridge of the nature trail.

Steep boulders are ascended into a narrow gorge, where the situation becomes more serious and the choice of route limited to finding the easiest passage. (It is possible to escape on the left at the start of this section, to avoid the main difficulties, but this diminishes the expedition.) There is an awkward ascent of mossy slabs on the left of the water to gain the lip of a long deep pool, hemmed by black walls. At its end is a two-step waterfall.

The crossing of this pool requires either a bold swim (the water

The entrance to Launchy Gill

stays cold even in summer!), an aqueous semi-climbing traverse of the right wall aided by an underwater ledge (if the handholds are wetted by the first across, the second will certainly fall in the pool!), or after the leader has crossed, a rope can be rigged with difficulty, for a Tyrolean. If the mossy rocks of the left wall are bone dry, then it is possible to traverse above the water, with some difficulty.

Once the pool has been conquered the situation remains exciting, where an impressive waterfall cascades over slabs. The climb, over slabs on its left, is easier than it appears, though a move past a small rock spike is awkward. A rope - and socks - are advised for this ascent. A short steep climb up the left branch of the stream reaches easier angled ground at the head of the fall.

Open scrambling continues to another impressive fall. Reach the base of this by slabs on the left, then along the water trough to creep round a pool at the foot of the fall. Escape from the gorge, with care, up a steep loose slope straight ahead.

Regain the stream bed at the top of the steep falls, for the scramble is not yet over. A short way above, the stream forks. Take the right-hand branch up a continuous rock staircase to finish through a dark ravine.

Descent: Leave the forest to gain the open moor. Follow the edge of the forest left, across the main stream of Launchy Gill, up and over a rise - deer are commonly seen hereabouts - to where the forest fence bends right. Cross into the forest and descend a leftwards sloping ramp to reach the end of the nature trail near the perched boulder - a good viewpoint over Thirlmere. Follow either branch of the trail back to the road.

88. DOB GILL   Grade 1   NY 316138

Dob Gill drains Harrop Tarn, a popular venue for a short walk up a forest trail. The gill is broad, with cascades near its top, and is used as an easy entertaining trip for large parties of young children. It is only feasible in low water when a lot of dry, rough rock is exposed.

Approach: Park just north of the stream at a forest car park. A trail leads into the woods, cross to the stream.

Character: A very easy grade 1, entirely over rough boulders in an attractive richly wooded setting.

The Route: Follow the stream bed, avoiding slippery rock and fallen trees. The top half lies to the left of the cascades.

89. WHELPSIDE GILL   Grade 1   NY 330139
This gill cuts a deep combe into the side of Helvellyn above Wythburn church.

Approach: Park at the Wythburn church car park near the head of Thirlmere. Take the steep well-worn path towards Helvellyn, up zig-zags to the end of forest. Contour left across the slight Combe Gill to reach the deep-cut valley of Whelpside Gill. Descend by the edge of the forest to gain the foot of cascades.

Character: A slight scramble in a fairly narrow watercourse which needs to be reasonably dry. However, who would expect to find such attractive cascade scenery so close to the boring tourist path? The rocks are slippery where wet or mossy.

The Route: Start at the foot of the cascades. Traverse the first pool on the right and escape up a grassy corner. Regain the lip of the fall to traverse clean rocks on the left side of the pool and climb stepped rocks on the left of the waterfall. Continue to a double cascade which falls over slippery mossy rocks. Clean dry slabs on the left offer a route, whilst the main fall may be feasible in drought. Regain the slabs of the stream bed. At the next cascade start on the right, make a slippery crossing of the pool lip to finish up drier rocks in the centre.
  The stream becomes bouldery with little scrambling interest. Either continue by a slight track at the side of the gill or traverse the hill to rejoin the crowds on the main Helvellyn path.

90. WHITESIDE GILL   Grade 1, 2 or 3   NY 318172

Another slight scramble which nevertheless provides a little interest on the way to Brown Cove. It is an insignificant gill which lies on the rocky hillside 400 yards north of Helvellyn Gill.

Approach: Park at the NWW Swirls car park below Helvellyn Gill. Cross the stream and take the path signed 'Sticks Pass.' Leave the main track at another sign to go left above the intake wall. Round the first spur reach a footbridge over a stream. Note the sign 'Do not pollute the water.'

Character: This narrow stream is noticeable in flood when a continuous white ribbon cascades over rocks. In drought it almost dries out, when it makes a reasonably interesting scramble which offers far more rock than the adjacent Helvellyn Gill and is the most interesting way to Brown Cove Crags. Slippery where wet or mossy. Too much water fills the available rock.

The Route: It starts well in a little ravine above the bridge, up the left side of a fall then straddles the narrow watercourse. Just above is the major difficulty of the trip where a tree guards access to a dark recess. Creep into the recess and if the water allows climb the steep, narrow, wet cleft at the back (3). The other alternatives are all shattered, so otherwise avoid the difficulty on the right. More amenable scrambling leads on. At a split in the stream the right channel offers most sport with small rock steps and slabs which culminate in a steeper barrier. Climb 10ft right of the fall to gain a shelf with a steep finish. The rocks peter out above.

Continue up the steep hillside to join a path which contours right into the base of the combe below Brown Cove Crags.

91. BROWN COVE CRAGS - STEPPED RIDGE   Grade 2**
NY 331161

The main central buttress of the crags gives a fine serious route, described in the previous *Scrambles*. This route is less serious, a good

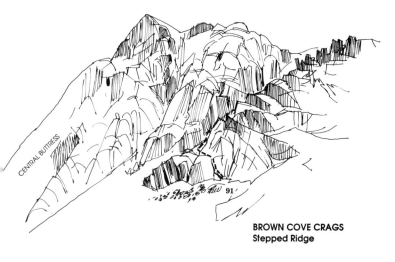

BROWN COVE CRAGS
Stepped Ridge

deal easier, but no less enjoyable.

Approach: By either Whiteside or Helvellyn gills, or the main tourist track up Helvellyn from Swirls car park.

Character: An easy-angled broad ridge with steep steps of rough grey rock. There are some loose flakes and perched blocks which demand judgement. A fine scramble, most difficulties can be avoided.

The Route: The foot of the ridge has a steep defensive barrier with rock climbing possibilities. The best scrambling route starts about 60ft right of the left edge of the barrier where a rock ramp slants left, delicate to start. This leads easily to the ridge crest. Keep close to the left edge up grass ledges and a rock wall to climb a rib which slants rightwards and is capped by a flat block. Pass your rucksack over the top and crawl under the block.

Continue up the broad ridge, most interesting close to the steep left edge which drops into the bounding gully. Keep left on a rock shelf overlooking the gully then move back right to the top of a slab glacis - care with some perched blocks! Move left again to an airy platform overlooking the edge and make a tricky exposed ascent onto the easier ridge above. A fine pitch on superb rough rock.

The next problem lies at a narrow neck with a steep wall above. Step down left, clasp an upright flake lovingly and mount carefully over a bunch of perched flakes to gain the ridge crest above. From the right climb shelves close to the left edge. At 20ft, faced with a smooth slab move right to a grass ledge. Regain the ridge. At the next rise cross a delicate slab left and step down to a ledge round the corner on the edge of the void. Make a steep ascent - care with loose flakes. Step from a sharp block to continue along the ridge. Pass through a block barrier to another block rib. Climb the left side of this to emerge on the top.

92. BIRKSIDE GILL   Grade 2*   NY 326125

Travellers over Dunmail Raise cannot fail to notice the attractive waterfalls in a gill close to the edge of the forest on the Thirlmere side of the pass. This is Birkside Gill which cuts a valley into the broad back of Nethermost and Dollywaggon Pikes.

Approach: Park on the grass verge of the southbound carriageway on top of Dunmail Raise close to Raise Beck. Cross a stile and take a permissive path left, signed 'Thirlmere.' This crosses a bridge on Raise Beck and leads just above the intake wall in half a mile to a footbridge over Birkside Gill.

Character: Continuously interesting scrambling on solid, rough rock more akin to Langdale than Helvellyn makes this an attractive, if short scramble. A succession of clear green pools and cascades in a slight ravine, feasible only in dry conditions. Save it for an hour to spare on a sunny afternoon.

Birkside Gill with too much water!

The Route: Enter a small ravine below the footbridge to traverse a deep pool and climb a slab on the right. Another pool is crossed above the bridge to reach a cascade. Continue to a steeper fall, climbed on the left and two more small cascades. After an easing of angle there are more cascades, the first guarded by a deep pool. Enter from the left and continue in the stream bed to a more formidable fall, its narrow channel impassable unless dried up. Avoid it left and regain the stream above. A broad rocky trough leads to a small steep fall whose mossy rocks are best avoided. Clean rocks on the left of a succession of small cascades lead to a narrow pool. Keep on the rocks right just above the water to gain a slabby trough ascended by straddling. Ahead is yet another deep pool backed by a striking cascade separated by a central rib from an overflow channel which provides a dry but sporting route. Move right near the top to finish up the central rib. This is the most serious pitch but good holds appear when most needed.

The angle relents as the stream cuts back into the hillside. A slight path descends the hillside diagonally back to the road.

93. NAB CRAGS: PERCHED BLOCK ROUTE   Grade 2
NY 314126

The long line of Nab Crags crown the right-hand side of the Wythburn Valley. This takes an easy-angled buttress which seems to offer the most continuous route, in the centre of the crags.

Approach: From Stenkin car park follow the permissive path on the north-west side of Wythburn. Pass below the buttress which can be identified by a sweep of slabs trending slightly rightwards. After half a mile, at the third stile, turn uphill by the wall. Go through a gate above the turn of the wall and make a way tortuously over a steep slope of bracken and rocks diagonally right to the foot of the slabs.

Character: After a messy start up vegetated rock the scramble improves. The pitch past the perched block makes the route worthwhile.

The Route: Start at a rib on the left side of the buttress, at a tiny tree. Climb the rib on steep earthy rock - care with holds. The next section is easier on better rock - straight up the left side of slabs to a large terrace below a formidable steep wall capped by overhangs. Note the perched block which juts above. Go round the left side to a groove which allows easy access to a ledge which traverses the buttress above the overhangs to reach the perched block. This is a very exposed pitch but is surprisingly easy. More slabs are climbed to the top of the buttress. On the left are two steep slabs which can be climbed to the ridge. The first slab is traversed diagonally left to right to finish up a crack.

The edge of the crags is an attractive place with fine views over Thirlmere and St. John's Vale. Descent can be made down the little valley at the back. At a flat shelf below a stone beacon on the ridge, an old pony track is joined, which zig-zags down to Stenkin.

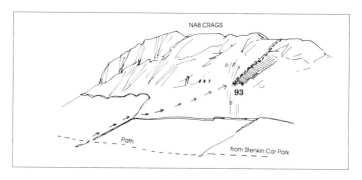

152

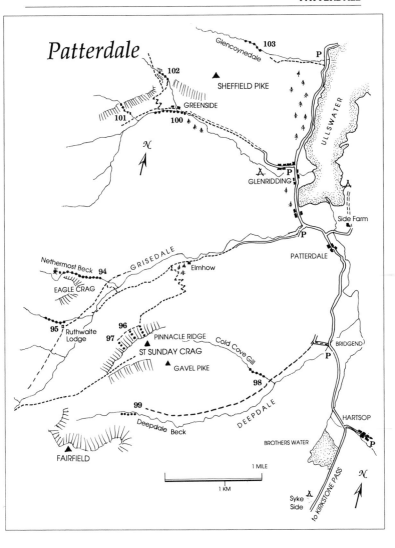

Patterdale

Patterdale

Patterdale with its many side valleys, encompasses a large area which includes several fine rocky fells. However, these are the eastern fells, whose rock is generally inferior in quality to the central and southern fells. Grass is abundant. Rare is the clean crag which ends in a fine rock platform. Often it is topped by a grassy fringe. Rock is sometimes spiky and shattered; green and greasy. If friction is good at times you are lucky, for more usually it is slippery smooth. Care is necessary on this type of rock. Crampon scratches are much in evidence for this is the domain of the dedicated winter climber.

St. Sunday Crag is the exception, for here the rock is reasonably clean and delightfully rough. Here is Pinnacle Ridge, probably the most classic scramble in the Lakes, clean as a picked bone and a prime example of what popularity does to a once adventurous route.

There are campsites at Sykeside (Brothers Water), Side Farm (at the head of Ullswater), and at Glenridding.

GRISEDALE

This attractive valley joins Patterdale almost at the head of Ullswater. Grisedale is a gateway to the fells; for the walker on Striding Edge, Fairfield and St. Sunday Crag; the winter climber in the coves of Helvellyn; or the visitor just out for a stroll up the valley. There is little to suit the modern rock climber here, but high on the north-west slopes of St. Sunday Crags is a wealth of easy-angled good quality rock which gives plenty of good scrambling.

Whilst St. Sunday Crag is the main attraction here, the streams which drain the coves opposite have their charms and are not at all serious.

Car parking at the entrance to the valley is limited and when full the car park at Glenridding is the best alternative, but adds another 1^1/2 miles on to the day.

94. NETHERMOST BECK   Grade 1   NY 358145
The stream which runs to the right of Eagle Crag.

Approach: Follow the lane up the valley for $3^1/2$ km. Past Elmhow it develops into a path. Dollywaggon Pike and Nethermost Pike appear as shapely cones above their respective coves, whilst Eagle Crag dominates the foreground. Just before Eagle Crag cross a footbridge and join a parallel path on the other side of the valley. Through a gate turn right by the wall to reach the stream.

Character: Nowhere serious, for the stream is not enclosed. There are numerous small cascades in a broad rock bed, but the trip is only worthwhile in a dry spell, when dry or water-washed rock can be used. Much of the rock is slimy and should be avoided. Care is needed. The route is open to choice and can be avoided anywhere.

The Route: The first cascade is climbed about 30ft right of the tree to find clean rock amongst the slime. At the next series of cascades go straight up the centre for 30ft then cross to less slimy rocks on the right. Regain the centre slabs. The angle eases. Follow slabs into a small defile and traverse the left wall.

Another set of cascades above are best climbed on the left. Amusement can be found as the rock bed continues, mainly at an easy-angle. One short fall has a clean rib on its left with an overhung base, but good finger holds. Some steeper steps end in a defile by a tree.

The stream scrambling is over but a knot of rock ahead can be incorporated at Grade 2. The holds are good but it is more exposed - by a slanting left to right ramp of slabs.

The flat base of Nethermost Cove is just ahead. High on the right is the crest of Striding Edge with a procession of ant-like figures. Perhaps the best continuation is by the ridge on the left which culminates in the rocky pyramid of Nethermost Pike.

95. RUTHWAITE BECK   Grade 2*   NY 355136
The next stream up the valley, by the old stone cabin of Ruthwaite Lodge.

Approach: As Nethermost Beck, but keep to the main path which mounts gently to the Lodge.

Character: More interesting than the preceding, although quite short. It has a short ravine and more of a true gill flavour. The rock is well supplied with holds, but where slimy is slippery. Keep to the dry bits.

The Route: A track leads into the gill from the hut, to an old mine level at the base of a cascade in a narrow ravine. The ascent of the left wall is the most difficult part of the trip. The stream cascades over the right wall of the ravine, too steep to climb, so exit on the right by a ledge, with a short descent at first.

Regain the stream, now a belt of slabs. Climb the right wall of a small defile and exit with the aid of a jutting tree. Slabs again, first on the right then the left. A series of steps lead into another defile, climbed on the left to a narrow trough which is awkward to surmount.

The final steep barrier lies ahead. Start up a slab on the right, cross a spray-lashed ledge to finish on the left.

ST. SUNDAY CRAG
High on the north-west slopes of St. Sunday Crag a long line of broken crags overlooks Grisedale. In the original *Scrambles* a description and enticing photograph of Pinnacle Ridge ensured that this route would become classic. Now there is a good path to the crag; the rocks of Pinnacle Ridge are clean and so well scratched by crampons of winter climbers as well as the countless feet of scramblers, that there is no longer any route finding to do - just follow the obvious way. The 'greasy groove' behind the Pinnacle is clean and many holds have been unearthed. Perhaps the grading should be reduced to 2, and every difficulty has a bypass path.

Haskett-Smith (1894) noted that the crags were long a favourite

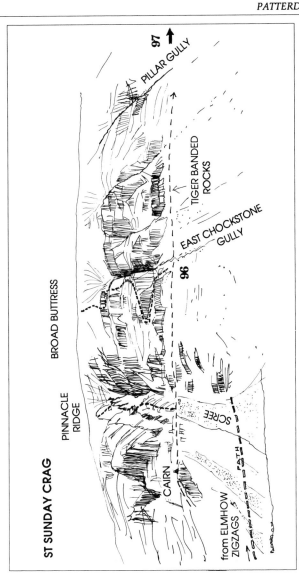

ST SUNDAY CRAG

PINNACLE RIDGE

BROAD BUTTRESS

PILLAR GULLY

TIGER BANDED ROCKS

EAST CHOCKSTONE GULLY

97

96

SCREE

CAIRN

PATH

from ELMHOW ZIGZAGS

scrambling ground of Major Cundill. Nothing further was recorded until the Sheffield climbers based on nearby Ruthwaite Lodge explored the crags in the mid 1950's. As a rock climbing arena it is too far to walk, and neither continuous nor steep enough for the modern rock athlete. Winter sees a transformation into a popular Alpine-style face with innumerable route permutations. If your taste in scrambling is to seek easy rock ways up what seems a large and complicated mountain face, then the following two routes will appeal. Combined with a descent of Pinnacle Ridge, it makes a fine mountaineering day.

Approach: Limited car parking up the lane at Grisedale Bridge, otherwise use the large car park at Glenridding. Follow the Grisedale road, which becomes a rough track, to Elmhow. At the far side of the plantation go left to pick up the Elmhow zig-zags, an old track which although steep, provides a pleasing smooth ascent. Where it reaches the floor of a combe there is a fork right which heads across the almost level shelf. Where it runs into steeper hillside ascend a little to a small reedy hollow. Keep left round this and up to a small but useful traversing path across the steep hillside. Cross two small scree shoots then a larger one which runs the full length to the crags at the foot of Pinnacle Ridge. Climb the steep slopes immediately right of this scree to a boulder shelf. Bear right to the foot of a deep gully - East Chockstone Gully. There is a small path which undulates below the length of the crags.

96. BROAD BUTTRESS   Grade 3**   NY 367138
This is the wide buttress between Pinnacle Ridge and East Chockstone Gully.

Approach: See above. The route starts at the right-hand corner of the buttress close to the gully.

Character: The scrambling is devious and intricate, with its share of loose blocks. Exposure is considerable in places and some people may require the protection of a rope at times. The lower band of steep

Grade 3 scrambling on Broad Buttress, St. Sunday Crag

dark grey rock is unsuitable for scrambling and the route seeks an easy way around this. Two steep areas of crag above succumb remarkably easily.

The Route: At the right end of the buttress between the bounding rib of the steep smooth slabs and the gully, is a lesser easy-angled light-coloured rib in the middle of a recess. Cairn. Climb the rib and slab on left of a corner to a grass shelf. Go left a few feet to the foot of a slabby rib of clean pale grey rock. At its base is a perched block. Climb the rib for six feet, then ease behind the block. Cross a steep wall to a rock ledge on the left. Continue up and left to a bilberry groove. Go up a rock step at the base of this and traverse 30ft left to a clean rib. Climb this and continue the traverse to easy ground. Ascend a short mossy wall to ledges. This completes the leftwards tour to avoid the steep band of dark grey, rather vegetated rock.

Return to the right edge of the buttress by a walk right along a bilberry shelf. Climb broken rocks just left of the edge to a groove. Climb a rib on the left to broken ground. Bear right towards the edge overlooking the gully.

A steeper crag looms above. Climb broken rocks about 50ft left of the edge and slant diagonally right into a recess with a huge perched block. Climb carefully between blocks to a rib of good rock to a bilberry platform. Ascend diagonally left towards a chimney, then diagonally right up into a groove. Climb this by the side of a block and exit on its top right. An exposed staircase on the edge of the gully leads to a boulder-strewn terrace.

The steep wall above presents several choices. One of the best ways is a rib which rises from square blocks just left of a slabby recess. Climb across a slab to reach the block and mount a 10ft crack to a flat-topped pedestal. A steep step above brings good holds and easy slopes.

On the left across the top of a gully is Pinnacle Ridge, an obvious crest of well used rock. This makes a fine descent if more scrambling is your choice. Sheep tracks cross the gully screes to the top of the ridge. Descent is straightforward although care is necessary (Gr.2). It is not easy to judge the stability of some of the numerous flakes from above.

For most enjoyment, seek the true rock scramble which more or less follows the crest. The descent of the steep groove into the gap behind the pinnacle is easier than it appears.

97. SOUTH-WEST BUTTRESS Grade 3** NY 365135

Another rambling route with a mountaineering atmosphere, based on the crags either side of West Chockstone Gully, which more or less bounds the crags on the right.

Approach: From Pinnacle Ridge follow the small path to the right below the crags. The first deep gully is East Chockstone Gully. To the right of this is a broad based buttress with the 'Tiger Banded Rocks' at its foot. Well up the crags are some tempting pinnacles, but the steep barrier of dark grey rock bars access. Continue the traverse past Pillar Gully and the very deep Y-Gully which hosts the best rock climbs on a steep crag at its back. West Chockstone Gully marks the end of the horizontal path, and the following route starts up the slabby rib on its left.

Character: The first pitch is the hardest, just on the verge of being true rock climbing. The steep rocks above, and the repulsive pitch in the gully, are avoided by a diversion onto the buttress on the right, to finish up the cleaner rocks on the left of the gully. Quite serious in places.

The Route: The rib is easy at first but holds become more sparse where the rock type changes. Keep just left of the edge and holds appear where needed. Step back right and finish up the edge to a bilberry terrace below an impending wall of crag.

Cross a ledge on the right wall of the gully to reach a grass ledge which leads into a smaller gully round the corner. Climb the slabby bed, move left onto slabs and avoid a bedded stone in the corner. The edge of the rib above is climbed dizzily, overlooking the gully. At its top there is an easy crossing of the gully to gain the attractive rocks on its left. Cross the gully, descending slightly to gain rock slabs on the far side. Climb these 30ft to a ledge left onto the buttress front.

Walk left along a flat narrow ledge to climb a rib below a jutting block. Below the block move right and ascend to a terrace. Climb a rib on the left.

The scrambling fizzles out into a bilberry hillside, although odd bits of rock can be incorporated on the way to the top.

98. COLD COVE GILL, DEEPDALE   Grade 1*   NY 391136

The stream which drains the eastern side of St. Sunday Crag makes its final descent into Deepdale over a very rocky bed.

Approach: Park by the telephone kiosk at Bridgend. Take a rough lane to Lanehead where the path up Deepdale goes left. After half a mile, just past Wallend Farm reach the open fell and the first stream of any consequence - Cold Cove Gill.

Character: Pleasant, very easy scrambling, often on broad slabs which if dry could be walked. Not at all serious, a good outing for novices. Excellent rock.

The Route: The scrambling starts at a holly tree a short distance above the main valley path. A stretch of broad slabs is followed by a slight ravine. Go up the waterchute close to the steep right wall. The ravine narrows and a short steep fall at its head is passed by a crawl along an overhung ledge on the right wall. Walking follows to another belt of slabs guarded by a short pool. Swing across the right side of this with the aid of tree branches, to gain the slabs which are climbed by their right side up a slippery chute. More walking leads to a final narrowing of the walls where a tree has recently slid across the stream. Cross the debris and climb awkwardly along the left wall to an abrupt finish.

Gavel Pike, the shapely outlier of St. Sunday Crag lies ahead, or the scrambles on St. Sunday Crag could be reached by crossing the col between it and Birks. Alternatively, return to the valley track by a path through the bracken on the south side of the stream and continue to the scrambles further up Deepdale.

99. DEEPDALE BECK   Grade 2*   NY 371125

Deepdale is a long, bare valley with a dramatic crag-ringed head; one of Lakeland's quieter spots. There are many scrambling possibilities, the best of which is Link Cove Beck which is described in the first volume of *Scrambles*. When approaching up the valley, the straight cut cleft which contains Link Cove Beck is mirrored by a similar cleft to the right where the main stream drops into the broad drumlin filled hollow of Mossydale. This cleft provides the scramble.

Approach: Park by the telephone kiosk at Bridgend and follow the main track up Deepdale for $2^{1}/4$ miles to the enchanting hollow of drumlins below the steep cone of Greenhow End. At the entrance of the rocky cleft, the main path rises steeply on the right.

Character: Not at all serious, but some ability is required to solve the various rock traverses above deep pools. Any difficulties can be avoided by an excursion out of the ravine, but this diminishes the fun. Good rock.

The Route: Climb slabs to enter the small ravine, which soon shows its character when the first deep pool is reached. Traverse the steep left wall on good holds. Pass the next pool on the right slabs and then one direct. It becomes easier but good sport is obtained by keeping close to the stream bed. At another pool, cross a ledge on the left wall, then cross the stream and ascend direct.

Now we are faced with a long deep pool with steep unwelcoming walls. It is easy to escape on the left and regain the stream bed above, but a strong party will cross the steep left wall which involves a bold swing round a prow just above the deepest part of the pool!

Ahead is another narrow pool, not quite so ferocious as the preceding but still quite intimidating. Start on the left wall then straddle across the deep water and shuffle into the safety of its narrows. Easier rock on the left of the stream emerges in the upper drumlin hollow below Hutable Crag.

THE GLENRIDDING VALLEY

The following short scrambles can be combined to make an interesting trip in a dry spell. Greenside is the old lead mining hamlet in the valley above Glenridding.

100. GREENSIDE RAVINE   Grade 1*   NY 366174

The main stream runs in a deep ravine just below the collection of houses. There is a particularly attractive waterfall, better than many a more famous one in the Lakes, but the only way to see it fully is from the bed of the ravine.

Approach: Either park in the large car park at Glenridding, or drive a little further up the narrow valley road to where traffic is barred just before a row of cottages. (In the winter months, cars are allowed as far as the mines, but the scrambles will normally carry too much water at that time of the year.) Walk up the mines road to Greenside, now an enclave of Outdoor Pursuits Centres. Gain the stream just before the houses.

Character: The river normally carries a strong flow which renders the expedition impossible, thus it is only feasible in a dry spell. Entertaining traverses on attractively water-sculpted rock are a feature of the trip. The main fall is impassable and must be avoided.

The Route: Scramble on whichever rock bank offers the most sport or indeed a way at all, to reach the first waterfall, which is passed easily on its left. The deeper gorge above is worth penetrating by a sporting ramp which undulates along the right wall to reach the lip of a deep pool, into which there drops a 60ft waterfall - one of the most hidden in the Lakes. Only part is visible from the track above. Unfortunately the pool and steep base of the fall are impassable; it is the sort of place where the French would fix a wire *fil de fer* to facilitate the passage, but of course here it is unthinkable. The only choice is to retrace steps along the ramp to broken ground and escape to the road. Just past a manhole cover you can regain the stream at the head of the fall.
  Traverse behind a tree and step down to gain a water-scoured

alcove. Climb out of this to a rib. Follow the attractive rock bed with a difficult stride over a deep inlet. Cross to the left to climb steep rocks to a weir. Final rocks are climbed under a bridge.

The next scramble lies up the small stream which pours over the lip of the craggy, juniper clad hillside on the right, a little further up the valley.

101. ROWTEN BECK   Grade 2*   NY 358172

Approach: Follow the path up the right side of the valley to a footbridge over the stream. Walk up the side of the stream to where it becomes scrambly at the right branch below slabs.

Character: Scrappy at first, it improves as height is gained.

The Route: Pass through a jungle of small juniper. Climb slabs, move into the stream then continue up a belt of water-worn slabs above. The main watercourse lies to the left and is best joined here to ascend a cascade. Continue up the steam in a slight defile. At a sharp bed the main scramble is revealed - a succession of three steep cascades topped by several minor steps. The first is 60ft, steep and mossy; the second a low barrier most easily climbed on the right. The third is another steep barrier best climbed on the left. Interest is maintained in the smaller cascades above.

The trip finishes on the edge of an escarpment. To reach the next scramble follow the escarpment back towards Greenside to join the path which comes from the hamlet to the upper mines before the deep-cut stream. Turn down the steep path to a cairn and take a small path left along a terrace above mine dereliction. Where the terrace ends the stream is easily gained.

102. STICKS GILL (East)   Grade 3**   NY 363178

Approach: As described above from the top of Rowten Gill, or by the Sticks Pass path from Greenside. This zig-zags up the steep hillside above old spoil heaps. The track crosses scree and at a cairn turns steeply uphill. Continue past the cairn along a horizontal terrace through mine dereliction above the stream. It is possible to see where an old bridge crossed the ravine to the continuation of the terrace. At the end of the terrace descend into the ravine.

Character: A short but interesting scramble up a steep-sided forbidding ravine. Only possible in low water. A short rope and a long sling prove useful.

The Route: Pass a timber weir on its right to gain the narrower upper part of the ravine. Climb a steep rib on the right wall for 15ft to a sapling, move left to reach easier ground. The next hazard is a deep pool with a delicate traverse across a steep wall. Climb to a platform. The waterfall ahead blocks the ravine but an escape can be made up the vertical left wall which has a series of good holds, the last of which proves to be shelving. It is easy to flick a sling over a spike above, which safeguards the move or can be used for aid. Cross the stream to finish on the right.

103. GLENCOYNE BECK   Grade 1

An interesting way up a quiet valley. Glencoynedale lies parallel and north of Glenridding. The scramble lies up a ravine in the middle section of the valley.

Approach: There is a car park just north of Glencoyne Bridge by the shore of Ullswater. Go over the bridge and take a lane right to Glencoyne Farm. A path continues up the valley, below the well named cottages of 'Seldom Seen.' The stream cuts through a well wooded ravine above.

Character: An attractively scenic scramble on slippery rock through a ravine unfortunately encumbered with many fallen trees. The stream bed is of solid rock with a succession of short cascades and falls. The rock on the side walls is shattered and should be treated with care. Perhaps best done in socks over trainers.

Trees are a natural hazard in Glencoyne Beck. Photo: A Evans

The Route: The ravine starts with some small cascades, but the obvious sporting traverse of the first pool on its left is dangerous - a jutting block is held only by tree roots. Climb easy risers as the stream twists in its verdant ravine. Several obstacles offer an easy way or a more sporting traverse of a steep wall. Just after a sharp left bend there is a steep, tricky traverse of the left wall over a deep pool (easily bypassed). A more formidable fall blocks the ravine. This is best avoided by leaving the gill about 100 yards below the fall by an easy-angled grass shelf leading rightwards. (The fall can be climbed with difficulty on the left but is loose and slippery.) The angle above is easy but the ravine is narrow and progress is a battle through a tangle of fallen trees. Force a way through to the final cascades but escape before them on the left.

104. HAYESWATER GILL   Grade 1 or 2*   NY 423130

This is a most unlikely setting for a scramble, as the valley seems hardly steep enough, yet it is surprisingly good. The stream drains the eastern side of High Street where a deep trench-like valley curls into the hills from Hartsop. Its ascent can enliven a walk to the tops.

Approach: Drive through the attractive little village of Hartsop to a car park. Follow the waterworks road up the north side of the main valley to a building where a path branches right across the river at a footbridge.

Character: The scramble is mainly in a low-walled, narrow ravine with occasional steps. The rock is excellent, although slippery where

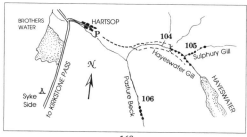

wet, and the scenery attractive with several beautiful pools. There are many water-worn *marmites* (a French word - cooking pot - which perfectly describes the circular cavities). Nowhere serious, you can choose whether to seek difficulties or avoid them. For best sport it needs at least a week of dry weather.

The Route: From the footbridge follow the stream bed past two slab barriers to enter a rocky defile. The first pool presents a tricky obstacle. If the rocks are dry enough, traverse the left side to climb a steep little wall in the waterflow to reach easier ground. Otherwise avoid this first steep wall by a detour out of the gill on the right to regain the rocks where the choice of route is wider. Another little defile soon follows. Traverse the steep left wall close to the water, with good handholds. The 15ft wide ravine culminates in an impressive circular pool backed by a cascade. In very dry conditions a direct route may be possible, but more usually an escape must be made up the left wall close to the entrance to the pool, by a steep zig-zag ascent around trees. The rock exit, on spiky holds, needs care.

Note the side-stream **Sulphury Gill** which enters on the left - a pleasant continuation after finishing with Hayeswater Gill. Walk a few yards up the main stream to another defile which contains a small cascade, climbed on either side.

Hayeswater lies a short way up the valley along the broad track which has accompanied the gill on the right. However, if further scrambling is desired, traverse the hillside on the left descending slightly to gain:

105. SULPHURY GILL   Grade 1
This is the side-stream already noted at the start of a long sweep of slabby rock.

There is plenty of choice on good staircase-like rock, perhaps the right-hand channel being the most interesting. Several rock steps prolong the scramble to easier angled slopes and join the path from Angle Tarn to High Street.

There are other gills of lesser interest on the steep eastern flank of

Hayeswater Gill beside **Sulphury Gill** which is the most rocky and open. The northernmost is the least interesting but has an earthy awkward step at mid-height. The central gill **Prison Gill** is merely a pleasant ravine with a few easy rock steps.

106. PASTURE BECK   Grade 1   NY 422115

Threshthwaite Mouth Glen is the steep-sided valley which joins Hayeswater Valley just above Hartsop. The most dominant feature of the valley is the fortress crag on the right - Raven Crag, Threshthwaite Cove - on which two difficult scrambles are noted in the previous guide. Below the crag the stream runs in a slight ravine which provides a short scramble on a walk up the valley.

The rock is good, with a striking band of òf pink quartz at one point. The way is obvious, any difficulties passed on the left.

Above the defile the valley opens into a broad cove rimmed by broken crags on which scrambling appears possible. However, the rocks are disjointed or too steep and scrambling here proves unsatisfactory.

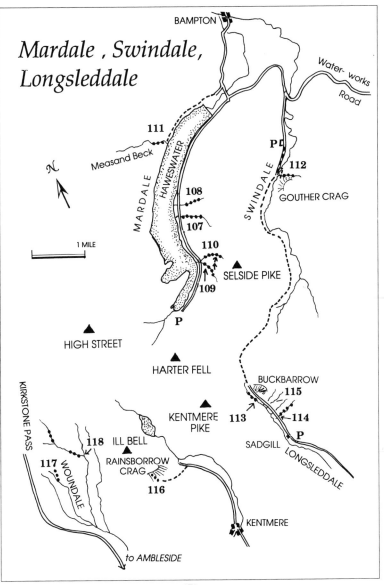

Mardale , Swindale, Longsleddale

BAMPTON

Water-works Road

111

Measand Beck

N

MARDALE

HAWESWATER

108

107

110

109

SELSIDE PIKE

P

SWINDALE

P

112

GOUTHER CRAG

1 MILE

HIGH STREET

HARTER FELL

KENTMERE PIKE

BUCKBARROW

115

113

114

P

SADGILL

LONGSLEDDALE

KIRKSTONE PASS

118

117

WOUNDALE

ILL BELL

RAINSBORROW CRAG

116

KENTMERE

to AMBLESIDE

Both these valleys offer little to the scrambler, for the eastern fells are less craggy than their counterparts in the central fells. The crags are generally scrappy and discontinuous, yet the routes described in Mardale are surprisingly good in the right conditions.

MARDALE

The following gill scrambles on the steep slopes which fall into Haweswater, can be combined to make a very good day at low water levels. They penetrate quiet hillsides well away from the popular paths at the valley head, and there are excellent views across the lake towards the High Street range.

107. GUERNESS GILL   Grade 2**   NY 481134

This is the second gill encountered south of Haweswater Hotel, which lies about half-way along the road overlooking the lake.

Approach: Best parking lies just past the gill where there is room to park off the road. Enter the stream by the bridge.

Character: The stream runs in a narrow, mossy, tree-lined ravine which cuts an almost straight trench up the hillside for a considerable distance. There are many cascades, pools and falls which give continuous good sport on rougher rock than is usually encountered hereabouts. The watercourse is narrow and needs to be fairly dry to enjoy the scrambling to the full.

The Route: The ravine starts almost immediately above the bridge and if the first stepped cascade can be climbed by the rocks on its left, then the water level should allow an enjoyable ascent.

The main ravine starts above with a delightful succession of little rock steps, pools and cascades in lush vegetated surroundings. The first real hazard is at a thin 30ft cascade. Climb the steep right wall on shelves with good holds. The innocent-looking mossy slab above on the left proves delicate to surmount. There is easier scrambling for a while, past several trees to a narrowing with a short but deep pool. In very dry conditions this could be forced - there is an underwater boulder which provides a useful stepping stone, but the subsequent ascent in the fall is slippery and lacking in holds. Usually it will be best avoided by an ascent of grass ledges on the steep left wall with a traverse back into the ravine above. Pass under a holly and along the side of a pool.

The easier gill ends at a sharp left bend where a 40ft waterfall is revealed. This makes a fine pitch by a rock groove left of the flow, dry in normal conditions. The holds are good but difficulties will increase if water has to be dealt with. There is an easy escape.

A path crosses the stream above but the ravine continues with good scrambling to pass below a water pipe at its top. The best scrambling ends here although you can continue further along the diminishing ravine.

108. GUERNESS WOOD GILL   Grade 1   NY 481136

This is the first stream encountered south of the Haweswater Hotel and only 200 yards from its worthy neighbour. It provides a slight but scenic scramble with easy walking interspersed with short mossy pitches around pools and small cascades.

The following two gills are highly recommended and lie nearer the head of Haweswater almost opposite the long spur of The Rigg which juts prominently into the lake.

109. HOPGILL BECK   Grade 2**   NY 481118

The main stream which cuts into Selside Pike is Rowantreethwaite Gill. Hopgill Beck is a less noticeable side-stream which runs in a narrow ravine. Both gills provide good sport and if Hopgill Beck is climbed first, the interesting upper part of Rowantreethwaite Gill is easily reached.

Approach: The road has widenings where a car may be parked close to the bridge, or better up the hill 100 yards north near the start of the Old Corpse Road, which was used by the villagers of the now submerged Mardale to take their dead to Shap before their own church was consecrated.

Character: Continuously interesting scrambling, at first in a verdant ravine, then on open rocks. It is only feasible in a dry spell. When the rocks are damp they are treacherously slippery and socks over trainers are advised. In a very dry spell there are a few slippery patches.

The Route: From the road bridge go through a gate and scramble easily up the rock bed of the main gill to the point where Hopgill Beck enters over a steep rock barrier on the right. Traverse the pool from the right and climb the steep rocks on the right of the lip of the fall. The holds are good. Pass two small mossy falls on the left to reach a much steeper fall over a jammed block. Bypass this on the left and re-enter the gill. Cross a pool on boulders to pass the next spout. The gill bends right to exit from the shadowy ravine.

Ahead the stream runs over rocks which afford good scrambling on slabs left of the flow. At the top of the slabs cross below a steep wall into the stream on good flake holds to gain a left-hand channel above.

A mossy fall guards entrance to another ravine. Pass it on the right over steep boulders. A deep pool is bypassed to regain the damp rocks of the gill. Pass the next fall by a dry route on the right. The gill continues past another cascade on the right and finally slabs on the left to finish by a large tree.

You can reach the interesting part of Rowantreethwaite Beck by traversing the hillside. Descend a very steep grass slope to gain the bed of the gill.

110, ROWANTREETHWAITE GILL   Grade 3** NY 480118
Approach: See above.

Character: The approach is hardly more than a walk; the climax a splendid serious pitch which requires low water conditions and perhaps socks over trainers for a safe ascent. Comparable with the main pitch in Ashness Gill, but easier.

The Route: The stream drops in a series of cascades, over the steep right-hand wall near the top of the main stony gill. Start on the right by a ramp round the back of a large sycamore. Or ascend more directly to reach the same ledge. From this ledge climb steep, stepped rocks with good tree root handholds, 30 feet to another ledge. The steep slabby groove above, on the right of the fall, is the crux of the route, exposed and quite tricky.

The situation eases and a dry overflow is climbed left of the next mossy fall. Pass the next cascade easily on its left and continue to meet a sheep track which crosses the gill where the scramble ends.

Descent: Follow the sheep track left across the head of the dry gill to a ruin where the Old Corpse Road is joined for a pleasant zig-zag descent to the road.

111. THE FORCES, SANDHILL KNOLL
Grade 1/2 NY 487155
Where Measand Beck discharges into Haweswater on its north-western shore is a prominent rock barrier over and through which flows a substantial stream.

Approach: Park at Burnbanks, the hamlet below the dam at the outlet to Haweswater. A well marked path runs above the cottages and along the lakeside to the stream.

Character: A frustrating scramble which is visually promising but proves a disappointment. Very slippery rock, best in socks over trainers. The gorge is a beautiful place worth visiting despite the quality of the scramble.

The Route: The stream forms a delta over broad easy-angled vegetated slabs, which provide a scrambly walk. Above, the stream flows through a high-walled gorge which can be waded or bypassed by a high traverse of the left wall.

SWINDALE

A quiet valley with a craggy head, Swindale's best scramble is Mosedale Force described in the parent volume. However, there are one or two other possibilities. Parking along the last two miles of road is not allowed and visitors must park before Swindale Foot, below Bewbarrow Crag.

112. GOUTHERCRAG GILL   Grade 1 or 2   NY 515129

The deep dog-leg ravine above Truss Gap Farm affords a slight bouldery scramble on slippery rock.

Approach: From the limit of parking walk about a mile along the lane to cross a footbridge over Swindale Beck just before Truss Gap. Take the path diagonally right to a footbridge at the base of the ravine.

The Route: Mount the broad bouldery floor of the ravine. Route can be varied to whim, best if the water level allows a direct route up the small cascades.

HOBGRUMBLE GILL which cuts a straight furrow down the steep wall of the valley head has caught many an eye. My party escaped from a mid-point after an unsatisfactory scramble up a narrow verdant ravine.

Longsleddale is one of Lakeland's quieter valleys, perhaps due to the very narrow access road which demands slow, careful driving. The head of the valley above Sadgill is wild and lonely, with broken crags on both sides. Few rocks climbers bother with the unfashionable crags, for the rock is not perfect. Yet Longsleddale can provide a pleasant day, in sharp contrast with the crowds of Central Lakeland. (See map p. 171)

113. RIVER SPRINT Grade 1 with a short section of 2   NY 478077
Hardly a true gill climb, for the height gain is modest, the River Sprint runs in a rocky bed below the quarry road where it passes Buckbarrow Crag.

Approach: Either park at Sadgill, or drive a further half mile or so up the rough road towards Buckbarrow. The best parking is on the verge when near a patch of firs in a circular enclosure on the right. Continue on foot along the road and when near the base of the crag go through a gate on the left, which gives access to the river. There is permissive access.

Character: The rocky stream bed runs in part in a slight ravine. A nice place to visit for a short diversion, especially if you like water-sculpted rock. There are many *marmites* (a french word meaning cooking pot' which describes perfectly the water worn basins). The bed is broad and solid, an indication of the amount of water which often flows here. Needless to say, it is only worth exploring in a dry spell. A pity the waterfall is impassable.

The Route: The walls close in to form a small ravine, guarded by a large boulder. You can easily surmount this on its left and penetrate to the foot of a spectacular fall with a jammed block. This would be a very difficult ascent even in drought, so return to the start of the ravine. There is an escape on the right, facing down, just above the large boulder, but on this side it is difficult to regain the stream above the fall. Make an escape on the left side lower downstream and try to re-enter the ravine just above the fall, where grass ledges lead into the stream.

Continue up the more open stream bed, with an interesting swarm across a flake which forms a little fall in mid-stream. Above is a double cascade; best ascended by rocks on its left. The upper cascade is more awkward and here the rocks are slippery, making an ascent in socks advisable. Cross the left wall into a recess and then escape steeply on good but slippery holds. The scramble fizzles out not far above. The upper cascade can also be surmounted by a good scramble up superb rough rock on the wall to its right. Start fairly far right beneath a sapling then climb a few feet and traverse left to exit up a short groove.

114. GALEFORTH GILL
Grade 1/2 lower section Grade 3s upper falls ** NY 484066
The eastern side of Longsleddale above Sadgill is steep and craggy. About mid-way between Sadgill and Buckbarrow Crag, Galeforth Gill flows over a lip of crag in a prominent waterfall.

Approach: The rough road above Sadgill is drivable at the time of writing, but cannot be relied upon. Probably best to park at Sadgill. About half a mile along the rough lane, just after a slight descent, go through a gate on the right. A prominent circular stand of trees on the hillside comes into view. Galeforth Gill lies just before this.

Character: A surprisingly continuous scramble on a good rough rock bed. Well worth doing as an easy scramble even if the challenge of the top falls is declined. As a complete trip it makes a satisfying after-noon. Rope advised. Overflow channels give a choice of route and make the gill feasible on a wet day if the flow is not too great.

The Route: The bed becomes rocky almost immediately with an introductory pitch at a small fall, or its overflow. Walking follows to the start of the main fare where the hillside steepens, and the scrambling is now almost continuous to beyond the top of the falls.

The rock strata is vertical which results in groovy flutings, quite pleasant to climb. A steep little climb just above the start leads into a narrowing with a waterchute, passable in dry conditions, or cross to a recess overflow in the right wall. Regain the gill to face another small fall climbed a few feet left of the water by a V-groove. Slabs left of the main stream are climbed by a parallel weakness to join the stream and a steep fall ascended on the right with the help of a tree.

An easing of angle brings the top falls into view, together with a change in the lie of the rock to a more slabby structure. In wet conditions socks may be necessary.

Climb the slabs left of the watercourse to a succession of rock steps in about 150ft of good scrambling towards the upper falls. There is a choice of route on the broad cascades. A steeper fall just below the upper falls is climbed by a right-left weakness to a rising shelf below the steep final barrier.

The scrambling now becomes much more serious and rope protection is advised. The main watercourse would provide a difficult pitch in dry conditions, but the route described takes the overflow channel in a V-groove left of the main stream. In wet conditions socks are advised. It is steep and awkward at about 25ft, nut runner, then move right 10ft to easier climbing up shelves which lead to a tree belay in about 80ft.

Various possibilities lie above, but the continuation of the overflow channel is steep, mossy and lacking in holds. Better is a grassy groove directly above the tree. This is steep and an obvious jug hold on its left wall is loose. Smaller holds in the crack are solid and the finishing holds are good. Another alternative is to cross the main stream by a descending shelf to the rib on its right. Mount a shelf by the side of a large detached and apparently unstable block. Step above the block to easy ground. Yet another way and probably the best of all if water conditions are favourable, is to ascend the main fall by a zig-zag route starting on its right.

Above the falls the scramble continues a short way before it peters out.

A slight path to the summit of Tarn Crag lies not far above; where the final crags afford a scrambling finish or descend well left of the main crag by a scree and grass gully. Alternatively a descent can be made to Sadgill via the craggy spur of Great Howe.

115. OTHER GILLS IN LONGSLEDDALE

Whilst Galeforth Gill is the best trip hereabouts, some of the other gills which cut through the steep craggy fellside have some interest. These are listed below:

1. NY 483071. The second gill north of Galeforth is a long one with a fork near the top. The bottom section is good with several interesting pitches which are not easily avoided. The culminating pitch of the lower section is topped by a capstone. The pitch is climbed on the left wall with a few moves up on good holds and an easy right traverse back into the bed of the gill at the top of the cascade. A good pitch. At the fork take the right-hand branch which though not so good as the lower section is worth doing. The rock is loose and spiky and should be treated with suspicion. If all the pitches are done this is a good grade 2.

2. NY 481076. The next gill north which comes down the fellside between Tarn Crag and Buckbarrow, is very easy. North again is this gill which runs parallel in the lower sections. This takes the scrambler through part of the broken upper ramparts of Buckbarrow Crag. The gill is quite long and starts easily with a series of wet, mossy pitches of increasing length and dampness. This continues with the gill remaining open and escapable until a more level section is reached. Here a broad shallow scree gully enters from the left, but the way is straight on up into a narrow, chimney-like cleft. At first the going is enclosed but easy. The stream which flows over the right wall of the chimney cannot be followed and so it is necessary to go further up into the chimney until it is possible to climb the right wall and then make an insecure exposed traverse rightwards onto easier ground. Further scrambling over broken rocks and steep grass complete the route. Grade 3 if done throughout.

3. NY 479079. The gill immediately north of the main body of Buckbarrow. It has one difficult pitch low down, then easy scrambling. Grade 1 or 2.

Rainsborrow Crag dominates the west side of the valley, a rambling mass of steep, mossy crag and bilberry ledges, which do not attract exploration. Other steep narrow gills on the eastern flank of Kentmere overlooking Ulstone Gill also prove unattractive. The sole scramble is described below.

116. RAINSBORROW CRAG, SOUTH GILL
Grade 3   NY 444064

On the southern side of Rainsborrow Crag is a straight-cut narrow cleft which hosts a tiny stream.

Approach: There is limited parking in Kentmere village close to the church although a new car park is under consideration. Take the private road up the valley, signed 'Hartrigg Farm.' This passes below the slabby rocks of Raven Crag (see the original *Scrambles*) and the steep outcrops of Calfhow Crag to pass Hartrigg Farm. The brooding vegetated Rainsborrow Crag comes into view and the cleft can be identified on its left side. Leave the road at the brow of a hill, just through a gate and walk to the foot of the cleft above the fell wall.

Character: Better than it looks, but there is some shattered rock and a fair share of vegetation. In poor conditions a rope is advised to protect several short but difficult pitches and the exposed grass escape. It follows a basically sound quartz vein which cuts through friable rock on each side.

The Route: Follow the stream bed to enter the cleft on the right. Several short pitches prove surprisingly awkward, to culminate in a steep little fall which can only be negotiated when dry. Escape left before this by a tree onto a steep grass slope. The ravine continues more easily above the fall.

The following are included for the sake of completion; nothing of great note but perhaps of interest if you are walking in the area.

117. HART CRAG, WOUNDALE   Grade 2   NY 412084

When approaching Kirkstone Pass from Troutbeck the road climbs out of the Troutbeck Valley and curves across the foot of a small upland valley. This is Woundale. A rough lane leads up the valley directly towards Hart Crag. A narrow gill gives easy scrambling before the rocks are reached. Hart Crag is more a series of smooth, steep, little walls which gives rock climbing problems according to taste.

118. HIGH BULL CRAG GILL   Grade 1   NY 423083

This stream falls into the top end of the Troutbeck Valley from the west. It is generally of easy angle and narrow with slippery rock. Not worth a special visit but it has a few interesting places. The gill is in two sections quite different in character and separated by about a third of a mile of boggy ground.

The start of the gill's lower section is just above its junction with Trout Beck. Take the left bifurcation. There are several easy pitches low down and more at mid-height with a short chimney and an awkward pool traverse followed by a steep wall. The scrambling peters out. The upper section is more enclosed but not steep, with some short pitches and traverses over pools.

119. SCANDALE HEAD GILL   Grade 2   NY 378094

At the head of Scandale a steep narrow rock gill is seen on the left. The rock is mediocre, the trip can be fairly wet if done direct. At mid-height the gill becomes enclosed. There is one awkward pitch, otherwise Grade 1.

Two small ravines on these otherwise smooth fells can add mild excitement to a walk.

120. BLEA GILL   Grade 1   NY 589029

A prominent deep-cut gill in the hillside below Winterscleugh. Probably best approached by the farm road from Greenholme. It is easy until about half-height where there are three pleasant pitches. The gill flattens but stages a recovery towards the end with two more pitches. The rock is variable in quality and friction (or lack of!).

121. BLACKLEY GILL   Grade 2   NY 583038

Can be reached by a short walk north from Blea Gill, or approached through the forestry plantation in Bretherdale.

The first pitch is a mossy groove, in the plantation about 100 yards below the fence. Next obstacle is the fence! Above is a wet pitch which looks formidable but goes reasonably if tackled direct. A couple more steps follow, the first best on the left, the second on the right. The next object of interest is a tractor which has been dumped in mid-stream. Best tacked direct - through the cab! Beyond this the gill levels with some small pitches. Rock is sound but mossy and slippery.

Index

		Grade	Star Grade	Route No.
ESK PIKE FORTRESS	Wasdale	2	*	69
ESK PIKE NW SPUR	Langdale	2	-	19
FAR HILL CRAG	Duddon	2	**	41
THE FORCES, SANDHILL KNOLL	Mardale	1/2	-	111
GAITKINS	Duddon	-	-	48
GAITSCALE GILL	Duddon	1	-	47
GALEFORTH GILL	Longsleddale	1/2	**	114
GATE GILL	Borrowdale	2/3	***	77
GILLCOVE CRAG - N.EDGE	Coniston	2	-	23
GLENCOYNE BECK	Patterdale	1	-	103
GOAT CRAG GILL	Thirlmere	2	-	85
GOUTHERCRAG GILL	Swindale	1or2	-	112
GRAINY GILL	Wasdale	2	-	67
GREAT END	Wasdale	2	*	68
GREAT GILL	Eskdale	2	*	55
GREAT ROUND HOW	Buttermere	2	-	74
GREEN CRAG	Eskdale	1/2	**	51
GREENSIDE RAVINE	Patterdale	1	*	100
GREY KNOTTS	Buttermere	1	-	75
GUERNESS GILL	Mardale	2	**	107
GUERNESS WOOD GILL	Mardale	1	-	108
HANGING KNOTTS GILL	Langdale	3	-	20
HARDKNOTT GILL	Duddon	1	-	43
HARRISON STICKLE				
South Central Buttress	Langdale	3	**	8
HART CRAG	Woundale	2	-	117
HARTER FELL, BRANDY CRAGS	Duddon	2	**	42
HAYESWATER GILL	Patterdale	1or2	*	104
HIGH BULL CRAG GILL	Troutbeck	1	-	118

		Grade	Star Grade	Route No.
RAINSBORROW CRAG, S.GILL	Kentmere	3	-	116
RAVEN NEST HOW	Duddon	2	**	40
RAVEN TOR	Coniston	3s	*	25
REDACRE GILL	Langdale	2	-	10
RED BECK	Borrowdale	3s	-	83
RED GILL	Eskdale	3	*	56
RED HOW	Duddon	1	*	46
RED PIKE from BLACK BECK	Wasdale	2	**	65
ROSSETT SLABS	Langdale	1	-	17
ROWANTREETHWAITE GILL	Mardale	3	**	110
ROWTEN BECK	Patterdale	2	*	101
RUTHWAITE BECK	Patterdale	2	*	95
SCAFELL S.E. SIDE	Eskdale	3	*	59
SCALECLOSE GILL	Borrowdale	1/2	**	78
SCALE GILL	Langdale	1or2	*	1
SCANDALE HEAD GILL	Outlying	2	-	119
SEAVY KNOTT	Ennerdale	3	*	72
SHUDDERSTONE HOW	Duddon	2	**	39
SIDE PIKE S.RIDGE	Langdale	1	-	9
SKULL GILL	Langdale	1or2	-	11
SLAB & NOTCH (Descent)	Ennerdale	3s	***	71
SLIGHT SIDE/HORN CRAG	Eskdale	2	-	62
SPOUT HEAD GILL	Wasdale	2or3	*	66
SPRINT, RIVER	Longsleddale	1/2	-	113
STAKE GILL	Langdale	1or2	**	12
STICKS GILL	Patterdale	3	**	102
ST. SUNDAY CRAG				
S.W.Buttress	Patterdale	3	**	97
Broad Buttress	Patterdale	3	**	96

Printed by Carnmor Print & Design, 95/97, London Road, Preston, Lancashire.